Lighten You

A journey to Natural Health and Well-being.

Learn to Discriminate

Practice your Willpower

Take Action

Hazel Humble

Natural Health Therapist, Healer and Facilitator

Disclaimer

The writings in this book are taken from my own thoughts, ideas and observations and are not in, any way, to be taken as absolute facts. I encourage you not to believe anything I have written but to seek the truth for yourself. It is through your own research and self-work that Inner Truth is found leading to Inner Peace.

In no event shall the author, Hazel Humble, be liable for any damages, from whatever cause, arising from any content in this book.

If you have a medical concern - have medical tests. Do your own research, ask questions until you have a satisfactory answer, and then make your own decisions.

Trust in yourself

The answers lie Within

© Copyright 2018 Hazel Humble
ISBN: 978-1-9164087-0-8

Printed by Book Printing UK
Remus House, Coltsfoot Drive, Peterborough, PE2 9BF

Cover image adapted from "Balloon Aircraft Air" by pngtree

Acknowledgements

Thanks to Cathy, my daughter, Astrologer and Teacher, for being instrumental in aspiring me to write, and for bringing order to my haphazard script. Thanks to Sadie, my daughter, Musician and Teacher for being yourself and sharing your achievements with me. Thanks to Josie, my daughter, Primate Rehabilitator and Plant-based Health Coach, for editing and encouraging me to finish. Thanks to Neal Kydd for the last minute graphics; without whose help, the book would have no cover. Special thanks to my Husband, Rick, for his patience and kindness throughout, and for helping with the technical production and final editing.

Thanks also to my Brother and Mentor, Roy, who has given me much support and shared many thoughts and insights.

Without my teachers along the way, I would never have got this far, or had the contents to share in this book. I thank you, Natalie Davenport for the Kinesiology training, Dinah Lawson for the Esoteric Healing training, and Jenni Shell for the Qabalah training. All of you gave me the foundations on which to build my life.

Thanks to the many friends and clients along the way who have added much richness to the tapestry.

Contents

Welcome

'Lighten Your Body' is an offshoot of a book I began to write, originally to be written in four parts; Physical, Emotional, Mental and Spiritual. During the writing process, I became aware that there was a need for guidance on the basics of our Being.

This book refers to the Physical, how to nourish, to bring the body back from sickness and dis-ease, and generally, how to maintain optimum balance. At the same time it was obvious that information was required, to give the backstory as to how mindsets, beliefs, traditions and habits have shaped our thinking.

With this in mind, I began to focus more on the physical. Questions became part of the process as we each have a different view of life, depending on our own peculiar circumstance.

There is much here that many may find debatable and it is this that has the ability to help open minds. As the mind becomes inquisitive, searching for answers, a link to the Deeper Part Within may be formed. Once accessed, much is seen in a more rounded way. The parts begin to make sense, once linked to the whole.

The realisation that memory is contained within every cell of the body makes the physical a powerhouse of information, from which we are able to release stress, negativity and dis-ease. The ability to create a positive attitude may be derived therefrom.

I trust that you will find the book informative enough to begin your own research into the realities that are hidden from sight.

Enjoy the journey and find, or expand, your own 'Happy Spark'.

Foreword

We have a mind, body and Soul. But if we overlook the body we are rejecting the very substance, given by our Creator, within which to work and progress.

The body is a Temple and in order to fulfil our mission, on this plane of existence, we have a duty to look after and maintain it, inside and out, just as we look after and maintain our physical home in which we reside.

The body gives us information about our physical well-being, our mental state and our relationship with our Soul.

As we learn the subtleness held within the physical body we are able to move forward with certainty, as a baby who learns to crawl, walk, climb, run and dance. New skills take time to master. Watch a baby learning to crawl, with determination to get onto the knees. After much practising, there he is one day, crawling to perfection.

His next step is to take him higher as he learns to walk. Again, after much practise and falling, walking is mastered. Every new experience has been challenging to the depths of his Being.

Taking the knocks and bruises in his stride he now learns to run. After much experimenting, he chooses to walk to reach his destination.

With steady surety he reaches his goal.

Background

I have been working with Energy Medicine for many years, improving health and life-style through the Physical, Emotional, Mental and Spiritual areas of Being, all equal to our health and welfare.

I trust you will enjoy reading this book, or page dipping. The pages may resonate with you, or something you read will trigger your own Inner Knowing. The third way is to use it as a workbook, working as you go. Keep a journal to answer questions for your own future reference. This will be an interesting project. Some time later, you can look back and review the positive changes made in your life.

There is no advice in these pages, no asking you to follow, but to look into your Heart, follow your Heart and take the Action you Know is Right..... Enjoy!

The Unexpected

The unexpected happens to us all, and it is these fragile times that are the greatest life changers. On looking back great gifts may be seen.

Unexpected events in life lead us forward to experience new challenges. This encourages immersion in new ways of thinking. Responsibilities come to the fore with the realisation that life is 'what we make it'. We have a choice to awaken the Inner Dimensions, our True Self, or drift with the crowd.

This phase of my life was instrumental in propelling me towards my life-work. It all began when my second daughter was about fifteen months. At this time her behaviour changed dramatically, screaming and crying at bedtime and also during the day. At bedtime she would rush around or bang her head on the cot. We held her to stop her hurting herself, or anyone else. Hugging or cuddling achieved nothing. There was no response. The loud cries were upsetting to anyone who could hear. Most people cannot bear the sound of shouting or loud crying. It is normal for us to want to find out why and help. There were minor physical symptoms such as stubborn cradle-cap, hot head and rashes.

Late one evening, hearing the loud crying, concerned passers-by knocked our door, calling through the letterbox, wondering what was going on. We opened the door. I was eight months with the third baby and carrying my inconsolable toddler. Having explained the situation to them the passers-by were relieved!! They had assumed she was on her own in the house. We were thankful to know that they cared.

As I was pregnant, my neighbour offered to take my daughter for the afternoons while I had a rest. My daughter played with her son of similar age. (Unbeknown to me, until some time later, all was not as quiet as it seemed.) I had been given the gift of peace and calm for an hour or so, for which I am forever grateful. Resting during that time helped immensely.

As time progressed there was no sense of fear. She would try to throw herself down the stairs. One day she actually managed it, when I was two steps farther away from her. She landed at the bottom, stood up and ran off. I immediately checked for any damage. Remarkably there was none except a lump on her forehead. Homeopathic Arnica was quickly given and the lump magically receded. Child gates were of no use now as she was quite able to climb.

I visited the GP who prescribed Phenergan, assuring me that there was something stronger if needed. He joked that I should invest in a padded room. The drug had the effect of making her sleepy during the day but not at night. Concerned that if we went back to the Dr., he would prescribe a stronger medicine, we decided to do our best to settle the behaviour without medical intervention.

I felt let-down by those I was brought up to revere. My faith in the medical profession disappeared, not for the first time, and was becoming a habit.

Nothing was effective. Nothing we did made much of an impression. We carried on doing the best we could. Crying loudly when taken out in the pushchair caused passers-by to mutter, "If that was my child", even though they had no answers. Three months later I gave birth to my third Daughter. Life was hectic. Every Mum knows about sleepless nights and you just get on with it, often in a daze. However, this was something else! Feeding the new baby at night was normal, but getting up for a toddler in between, was exhausting. Fortunately my new baby was calm and happy and seemed undisturbed settling to regular feeds and sleeps very quickly.

My husband, although in a high pressured job, helped considerably. We took it in turns to get up every night and stay with her. This continued for the next two years. How Rick did it and go to work, I have no idea. When he came in from work, he would take over and I would go and see a friend who lived just round the corner. I would stay for half an hour whilst she prepared her evening meal. I would then return home and serve the meal I had prepared earlier. This break was my saving grace. No-one, except my friend round the corner and my former neighbour, knew the turmoil we went through.

One day I read in the local paper an article about a boy who was sensitive to Cow's Milk. The article was written by a member of the Hyperactive Children's Support Group. The information described my Daughter's behaviour! Following my instinct, I made the decision to stop all Cow's milk for my little girl.

I found a local farm that sold Goat's milk and changed to that. The next four days were horrendous, the behaviour and crying accentuated. Instinct told me that this change was part of the process. The fifth day she sat on my lap, looked into my eyes and smiled....... This was unusual, and to be able to give her a cuddle too........ That night she went to bed and slept right through until the morning. Needless to say, I was up every half hour during the night to check she was okay!

Thankful that we were on track we proceeded with calmness. During the recovery from Cow's milk sensitivity there was the odd mistake when cow's milk was ingested. On one occurrence she had a tiny bite of a fruit pie and all the symptoms returned. The only milk in the pie was on top where it had been basted – no more than a drop could have been eaten. It took a few days for the reaction to pass. There were still factors such as habitual behaviour, or 'trying it on' when a glint in the eye would give it away. These factors were important to take into consideration. Once we knew what to look for, steps were taken to clear the behavioural residue as much as possible. The formative years, under five, are very important and I was concerned that our daughter was losing the training and learning that takes place during that time. So I did all I could to help her catch-up. This episode of my life lead me to investigate further.

I contacted the Hyperactive Children's Support Group and became a member, attending meetings and running support groups for parents with similar challenges. The key place to start, for many, was the Feingold Diet that excluded all artificial additives such as colourings, preservatives and flavourings. During this time I was introduced to Touch For Health, the method upon which all Kinesiologies are based, and realised very quickly, that I could be of service to many with this wonderful tool that allowed detection of sensitivities/allergies. Enquiring further, I found more information and immediately prepared to use this knowledge to help the members of my groups. Seeing excellent results, they encouraged me to set up a practice, which I did.

The Allergy Detection and Natural Healing Centre was born.

This is how I was guided towards my passion for health and healing. I trust this book will help you find your own passion for Life and Living.

Part 1

The Number One Offender

"Cow's milk and dairy products are not essential for health – in fact they do more harm than good."

Juliet Gellatley, BSc, Dip CNM, NTCC founder of Viva!

It is no surprise that we begin here! Cow's milk is the number one offender that keeps the body 'heavy'. This I see in my practice, and there is much information as to why that should be so......

Cow's milk and associated products

Many diseases are linked to Cow's milk. We have been led to believe that Cow milk, cheese, cream and yogurt are essential for health but research shows the reverse to be true.

- These products contain saturated fats, proteins, hormones and antibiotics.
- Growth factors such as IGF-1 increase in the body, and are factors much linked to cancer.

In my experience, I have found many changes take place when Cow's milk is removed from the diet.

However, any substance – eaten, drunk, airborne or topical can cause reactions or sensitivities.

From birth and all through life the body and mind are affected by foods and drink. Feeling under the weather or not quite right becomes a daily mantra. Eventually a diagnosis is searched out, becoming the focus and concern. Once given a diagnosis, unquestioning acceptance of medical treatment often ensues.

Each living being on our planet knows how to survive and which foods to consume to keep them healthy; all except humans that is. Every illness, disease and mental issue can be helped or even eradicated by knowing the foods that help or hinder.

The mid 20th century saw manufacturers changing natural foods beyond all recognition. Clever advertising of their products giving the impression of healthy choices. Yet, the content includes chemicals, colourings, preservatives and flavourings, many carcinogenic.

2

The animal agriculture businesses use many drugs including antibiotics and growth hormones. 75% of antibiotics produced are fed to animals within the industry. These drugs and chemicals enter the body of humans, when consuming animal flesh, creating havoc with natural body bio-chemicals and creating resistance to life-saving drugs - the drugs needed for emergencies.

It is no surprise that many foods create or worsen dis-ease. Addictive factors causing cravings and bombardment by false advertising, give the impression that these unnatural foods are full of nutrients needed for health.

Dairy, sugar, crisps, chips, white bread, alcohol, sweets, chocolate and meats make us crave. The lack of nutrients in these foods causes the body to remain 'hungry' and creates acidity. Fooled into thinking the body needs more food, more of the same is ingested allowing the cycle to continue. Even added vitamins and minerals are synthetic and not fully absorbed.

Think about it for a moment - the fruit and vegetable counter with all the wonderful colours makes your mouth salivate at the sight. Unfortunately the craving for foods that are harmful is strong, so foods that satisfy the craving are purchased. The plea from the body is perilously ignored.

Allergy/sensitivity and addiction go hand in hand making for a complex situation, easily overcome once you know how to take the necessary action. Often times there is more than one unrecognised addiction as the body becomes more and more sensitive.

The irony is, you know you are not eating healthily or supplying the body with wholesome nutrients.

Imagine you are tested for allergy/sensitivity and asked which food or drink would be most challenging to stop. The key item shown from the test is, usually, the same as your answer. Strong beliefs had interfered with your Knowing -

- Believing that your system is identical to others.

- Belief in misleading information.

- Belief that your body will accommodate anything put into it.

3

- Belief that it must be okay, because you have consumed the same food or drink since childhood.

Becoming aware of addictive behaviours, and allergies enables steps to 'clear' them. Not only your physical body is healthier and pain free, but mental and emotional torments lessen.

Imbalances caused through foods and drinks are known to amplify pains and hurts. Feeling 'better' in the moment after food or drink, leads to a down point causing the system to bounce from one extreme to another.

It is easy to see why behaviours suddenly change. That satisfying feeling after a bar of chocolate, a piece of cheese, a pork pie or glass of wine exacerbates emotional, mental or physical symptoms. These appear when the stimulation ceases.

When exposed to continual information such as news and media, it is easy to 'believe' all is real and true. This stops your own action and necessary progress.

Tiny, everyday occurrences call to be seen and heard, cleansed and released.

An example of behaviour simply corrected with dietary changes:

Mr. Y. A man in his mid-twenties, came for an allergy test. He had several motor-bike accidents, had been in trouble, was despondent and his behaviour was 'out of control'. He had been a lively child, had ADHD and in his teens started drinking heavily. He was desperate as he knew he would end up in 'big trouble' if he carried on in the same way.

Testing revealed sensitivities to all chemical colourings and flavourings as well as cow's milk.

Mr. Y lived alone in a bed-sit. He went home, cleared his cupboards and bought only foods that were natural. As suggested, he ate three meals a day. He cut out junk containing chemicals and all products from the cow. Two weeks later a smart, calm young man walked into my clinic. He had changed his diet completely, eating three good meals a day. Snacking in between had stopped. This he found much less expensive than before. His friends were astonished, not only at his calmness, but also the way he was eating 'like a King' and being able to afford such luxury – as three meals a day!!

4

An example of ill-effects on the physical body:

Mrs. X. Came for an allergy test hardly able to walk, using crutches and helped by a friend. Feeling trapped and frustrated, she had been diagnosed with Myasthenia Gravis - a neuromuscular disease affecting the muscles and breathing.

The main sensitivities were beef, pork and lamb. She stopped the intake of all meat and related products such as cow-milk. Returning two weeks later – she walked unaided. All symptoms had diminished. In the medical world, remission is the name for such a transformation. As long as the diet continued all was well.

Symptoms/Diseases

Addictions have become so much a part of life that they go unrecognised. You can be addicted to anything, not only drugs and alcohol. Sugar, wheat, dairy and animal products are high on the list. Because they are being consumed daily and always have been, it seems unfathomable that they could be 'quietly' harmful.

Symptoms and diseases are aggravated by the food and drink you consume.

When you put the wrong fuel in your car, what does it do?

The answer is, it doesn't work and parts are damaged.

This is no different for the body.

The right fuel gives a healthy body.

Wrong fuel produces an unhealthy body.

As physical beings we are more complex, and other factors come into play such as hereditary factors and stress. However, the one thing you have control over is the food and drink you choose to consume.

Following is a list of familiar symptoms/diseases caused or aggravated by the wrong 'fuel', there are many more:

Hay-fever, asthma, breathing problems, migraine, depression,

hyperactivity/ADHD/Autism and behavioural problems,

rashes, arthritis, constipation, diarrhoea, ear infections,

tonsillitis, obesity, irritable bowel syndrome,

candida and yeast infections,

menstruation problems, sugar craving, rheumatold arthritis,

muscle pain, menopause, auto-immune disease such as M.E.,

fibromyalgia and chronic fatigue syndrome

to name but a few.

A little more on Behaviour as there are many varied symptoms:

Cot rocking, head banging. Walking on toes.

Poor sleeping or crying out in sleep.

Abnormal thirst. Compulsive aggression.

Disruption at school or home.

Lack of concentration. Scratching or biting.

Clumsy, poor eye/hand co-ordination.

Speech difficulties. Dyslexia.

Memory deficits. Poor comprehension.....

These symptoms also affect adults.

Hay-fever - Asthma and breathing problems are subject to the same:

Once caused by grass and hay, hence the name. Grass, pollens, tree pollen, dusts, animal fur and feathers are quite common.

Today there is the added pollution from:

Heavy traffic with exhaust fumes and diesel. Pesticides, herbicides and factories - accounting for thousands of toxins in the air. In the home there may be moulds, gas, perfumes, air fresheners and tobacco smoke.

Hay-fever is correctable once the offending factors are identified. Using Energetic Medicine, identification is immediate with no side effects.

Once again, diet plays a part. Cow milk, wheat and sugar exacerbate the condition whilst a purely plant-based diet, cleanses the body, taking with it many symptoms.

Animal milks are noted for creating congestion in the form of mucus or catarrh throughout the body. This is unhelpful as the body has to struggle to breathe, firstly because of the milks and secondly because of the grass (also ingested by the cow from whence came the milk!)

Medicines suppress, without ever stopping the hay-fever, ensuring it arrives every season.

Watery, itchy eyes, running nose, sneezing, wheezing and rashes are all symptoms of hay-fever.

Most people wait until the season begins before seeking advice. This is not the wisest option.

Energy Medicine has the answers at any time of year to lessen and prevent outbreaks.

Take a step nearer your Goal!

Eating clean, lighter, non-acid forming foods and cutting out the junk allows the body to rest easy. This helps the move toward better physical, emotional and mental health.

The body undergoes changes and reaches it's own level and natural bodyweight. Fluctuations from high to low desist. Blood sugar levels stabilize and the body breathes calmly. The strain and struggle with foods that are unsuitable for your digestive system, no longer happens.

This step is of tremendous healing on all levels. Prevention is key.

One of my favourite sayings is:

'Prevention is better than Cure'

and how true is that when health is involved.

Interestingly, when you are sick the body automatically yearns for fresh fruits. Our, usually lost, instincts come into play.

Fruit juices and smoothies are gentle and grapes have long been given to patients at home or in hospital, whilst vegetable soups are kind to the digestive system, warm and comforting.

Food and digestion

Humans are able to eat and absorb all necessary nutrients, including protein, from the food groups shown later. Digestion begins in the mouth continuing with the stomach. It then follows the very long small intestine eventually entering the large intestine. This enables absorption of nutrients at each stage, taking several hours.

Carnivores, have a very short intestine, enabling the consumed animal meat to pass quickly through. It has no time to putrefy and harm their bodies. Carnivores pass the meat through the body almost as soon as they have eaten.

What does meat do to the human, long complex intestines?

Write in your Journal.

The Digestive System and it's Importance in Health

- a more detailed look

Digestion starts with sight, smell and taste, alerting the body to expect food. Salivation occurs next, preparing for what is to come. The digestive process begins in the mouth. The teeth masticate the food. The chewing excites the salivary glands even more, demonstrating the importance of the process. Thorough chewing creates a healthy digestive system, promoting the flow of digestive juices.

The stomach is the most important organ of digestion. Mucous membranes line the walls and secrete gastric juices to further break down the chewed food. Nerves are in abundance here and have a powerful effect on the whole nervous system. Therefore, when the stomach is under the influence of disease, either acute or chronic, the whole system is immediately in a state of suffering. It is therefore vital to keep the stomach healthy.

The liver provides the bile. It is the largest gland in the body. It gathers and carries out of the system substances that, if retained, would prove harmful. When the liver is not functioning correctly, jaundice occurs. When this is the case, a yellow hue appears in the white of the eyes, and sometimes covers the surface of the whole body.

The bile, when properly secreted and discharged, meets the contents of the stomach as discharged into that part of the bowels nearest the stomach. Separation of the nutritious part of the contents from the refuse which is passing to the bowels is it's purpose; but its more important purpose is to aid the passage of the faeces, by evacuation. The bile seems to be nature's appropriate stimulus to the bowels.

The bowels contain vessels, which absorb and, take up the nutritious part of food, transporting it to the blood and supporting the system. They also carry the refuse part of food out of the body.

This conveys the lengthy process involved for foods to be absorbed into the system, taking nourishment at every stage.

(Extreme pressure is put on the digestive system when a large, stodgy, acidic meal is taken. The body working at optimum to expel the unwanted matter and confused at the lack of correct nutrients. This then has the body asking for more nourishment. So, very soon, you are hungry once more.)

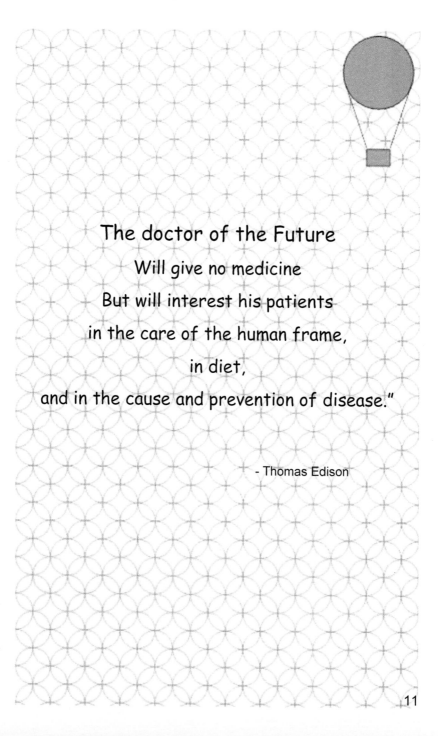

The doctor of the Future

Will give no medicine

But will interest his patients

in the care of the human frame,

in diet,

and in the cause and prevention of disease."

\- Thomas Edison

Part 2

Drinking loads and Dehydrated!

Water is the basic necessity for life.

Without water we cease to exist.

Water comprises the major part of the blood serum and every tissue and organ.

Many people are dehydrated without ever knowing. However, the body tells the tale by creating dis-ease within the body.

When sufficient water is not absorbed, the stomach secretes an excess of hydrochloric acid. This occurs particularly whilst eating foods that lack moisture. Fruits, are rich in moisture. The strength of the acid has a tendency to crystallize starch causing blood crystals. This is one of the primary causes of rheumatism, gout, lumbago, arterial sclerosis (hardening of the arteries), and all disorders caused by congestion throughout the capillary and arterial systems. One of the most common disorders among 'civilized' people is hydrochloric acid fermentation.

This is why when we are sick our body lets us know that we need water. Teas, coffees, sugary drinks etc. suddenly lose their appeal.

Many health problems cease to exist by changing the regular drink from tea or coffee to water. Sugars, aspartame, preservatives, colourings and chemical additives are found in most canned and bottled drinks. Coffee and black tea contain caffeine, a stimulant that can be addictive.

Unfortunately, tap water contains a range of chemicals used to control bacteria and other substances. As well as killing bacteria, these chemicals can be harmful to you. A water filter or bottled water is better. You can choose glass bottles instead of plastic to keep pollution down, saving oceans, fish, animals and ultimately yourself. Do the best you can depending on where you live.

The latest research shows that much information, often thought of as 'old wives tales', is correct.

Certain ways of eating and drinking are healthier for us, enabling water to be utilized in the optimum way. When we look at people who live in the desert, we wonder how they survive without water. They eat plants, and intake the fluid they need in this way.

Standing water in the sunlight helps absorbability – not in a plastic container as the water will be contaminated with chemicals from the plastic.

Easy ways to rehydrate:

- Vegetable Soup is more hydrating than water, given always when someone is sick.
- An apple and a bottle of water rehydrate better than two bottles of water.
- Drink smoothies rich in plants.
- Green juices squeeze out the water from inside the plants, direct from plant cells to your cells.
- Eat foods that contain water.

(Eating a plant-based diet with plenty of fruits and veggies is naturally hydrating.)

Since living in Spain, I discovered that watermelon is more hydrating than water. This is eaten in the summer by the locals, considered essential, containing many nutrients including micro-minerals.

- Add a pinch of Himalayan Salt to water to gain more micro-minerals.
- Grounding helps the absorption of water.
- Walking barefoot on the grass or by the sea keeps the body negatively charged.
- Antioxidants, Probiotics, Coco Water and Basil/Tulsi increase the availability.
- Moving exercise helps the water to be absorbed further into the tissues.

H3O2 is an essential part of water, also known as EZY water or structured water.

H3O2 is negatively charged and works to rid the body of the positive.

Not so good is swimming pool water containing chlorine. You may find you have a sense of dryness when leaving the pool unlike when you entered.

'Round-up' actually decreases the amount of EZY or good water. Round-up is still sprayed on many crops depleting them of their own natural health giving properties.

When under stress more hydration is required by the body.

Extra hydration is required when studying, taking exams or exercise etc.

Before massage, healing session or meditation, it is wise to drink a glass of water to help the energy to circulate, the same as before any form of exercise.

The more energy used, the more water, juices and smoothies are naturally required.

Dehydration takes place very quickly, particularly in the heat – indoors or out - or when travelling by car or aeroplane. So be prepared.

For more information on H302 see the 'Hydration Foundation' from whence this was taken.

Toxic Build-up

Our bodies are capable of adjusting to many changes over long periods of time but are unable to adapt to the thousands of changes that have taken place during the last seventy years or so. We are bombarded with drugs for every trivial ache or pain and injected with poisons at the hint of a new virus. This encourages the body not to fight and has the effect of depleting the immune system.

Substances include:

- Metals, chemicals and exhaust fumes pollute the air.
- Denatured foods full of pesticides and herbicides.
- Processed foods in packets - sweet or savoury - differentiated only by added flavourings, sugar and highly refined seasoning.
- Preservatives, additives of all kinds and colourings, known to be carcinogenic, used in sweets, crisps, cakes and soft drinks.
- Antibiotics and growth hormones are ingested every time animal meat is eaten or dairy products consumed.

- Planting is no longer natural. Huge areas of land are planted with one species (monoculture) upsetting the ecological system and killing insects, birds and animals.

The work these mini-beasts do in their effort to preserve the land is exquisite.

All have their place and job to do in nature even though many do not have the vision to see.

- Yet, man uses killer concoctions of herbicides and pesticides, killing the creatures, and himself in the process, by changing the perfect order of nature that has existed since life began on this planet.
- The rise of technology, chemical drugs, factory pollutants, plastics, decimation of forests, plants, animals, birds and sea-life has made a huge impact on how we view life.
- Many live inside houses with little or no ventilation.
- Artificial fresheners sweeten the air, chemicals from new carpets, clothes and furniture fill the air with the residue of fumes.
- Spraying the body with perfumes, aftershave and deodorants add to the mix, travelling through the air, much further than imagined.
- Gels and hairsprays are used on the head.
- Covering the face and body with creams, lotions, potions and sunscreen full of chemicals. Many face creams contain Collagen..

Where do substances such as collagen come from?

Yes! Medical and Cosmetic collagen come from cows and humans! So that filler on the face – ugh!   ...   Which human was it taken from - think about it!!

Those who are able to see

beyond the SHADOWS and lies

of their CULTURE

will never be understood,

let alone believed, by the

MASSES

— Plato

Natural products

In order to keep the home spotlessly clean, bottles and bottles of cleaning products are purchased, each one full of toxic chemicals and highly perfumed.

This is one way I find the use of Essential Oils a blessing, antibacterial at the same time. A few drops of Mint, Eucalyptus and Tea-tree Oil are some of my favourites, when cleaning or dusting. This method also negates the use of Air-fresheners loaded with toxic chemicals.

- Dusting - a damp cloth with 3 or 4 drops of oil gives a great aroma. Damp dusting is safer for people with allergies as dust stays on the duster instead of flying back into the air! Make sure oils are tolerated, or use water on its own.

- Natural Disinfectant may be simply made from essential oils; Tea Tree, Mint and Eucalyptus, mentioned previously. These have many uses in the home, are antibacterial and deter insects. Add a few drops of oil to 500 ml hot water. Add 2 tbsp. White vinegar. Shake well and then add a little washing up liquid. Spray on and gently wipe off. Suitable for most surfaces. If uncertain, test a small area first to be sure.

Laundry is washed with a chemical detergent and then softened with yet another product because the detergent makes the washing rough.

- An Eco Washball, available in Health Shops and some supermarkets is efficient. The Ball does not need any additions, no detergent and no softener. It is also inexpensive. One re-usable product, no cardboard waste, no chemicals to harm the skin and environment and no plastic bottles! Mine was on special offer and cost less than one pack of detergent – it is still in use after many years - a huge saving as an added bonus, as well as helping the environment.

- Soap Nuts is another natural product. Although called Soap Nuts they are really Berries. This may be one of the oldest ways of cleaning clothes. This product may be used alone or with a little washing soda for deeper stains. *For more information, and how to use: see 'References' at the end of the book.*

- A few drops of any Essential Oil, of choice, may be added to the rinse cycle if you so desire.

- If the washing needs extra cleaning, there are eco-friendly soap powders, or washing soda, mentioned above. Having many other uses, washing soda is especially useful for cutting through grease.

Carpets are manufactured with at least 40 chemicals.

A new car or office building can cause severe lethargy, tiredness and sickness, because of the chemical content taking many months to dissipate. Some things are out of your control but many are within your hands.

- For a new carpet, keep the windows open for several days before using the room, or as long as you are able. Keep the windows of a new car open for as long as possible.

Chemical aromas in air-fresheners wreak havoc with Asthma, hay-fever and breathing problems.

- Solution – let in some fresh-air or burn essential oils such as lemon grass or mint for a fresh aroma or use incense sticks. If someone in the house has any of the above symptoms, be cautious.

- Fresh lemon or mint in a pot of hot water produces a gentle aroma and is generally tolerated.

Window cleaners, mould removers, disinfectants, floor cleaners, polishes. There are natural alternatives to these.

- Window and mirror cleaner – 3 tbsp. White vinegar, 500 ml water and a few drops of washing up liquid.

- Insect prevention - the above recipe may be used to spray the soil and plants.

Vinegar has many uses. Here is another:

- Mould Remover and Limescale Remover – Use equal parts of water and white vinegar. Spray on to the area, leave for a while, then wipe off.

Personal products – shampoos, conditioners, shower gels, perfumes, deodorants, hairsprays, mouth washes and more.

- A home-made toothpaste is simply made from organic coconut oil and organic turmeric. This I make in a tiny jam-jar, filling ¾ with oil, then stirring in about 1 teaspoonful of turmeric. Set in the fridge. Use the end of a teaspoon to remove the toothpaste and apply to the brush. (It is not so easy to use when it has warmed and liquefied, so is best kept in the fridge!)

This mix I also use on the skin for blemishes and as a face-mask. Be careful as the colour stains clothes, towels etc. However, it is easily wiped from the skin. Be cautious and leave on for a couple of minutes at first. When you are satisfied, you are not going to look as though you are severely jaundiced, gradually lengthen the time.

• A Natural Deodorant Salt Crystal may be used instead of chemical laden deodorant sprays, roll-ons or anti-perspirants.

Search for animal friendly products containing natural ingredients and aromas. There are many available from Health Shops.

There are many other ways such as using fresh lemons for cleaning and for the skin. Many products have a lemon aroma but contain only chemicals. Lemon is antibacterial and is useful for cleaning chopping boards, a squeeze in the washing up water etc.

The hunt for lost cherished items!

Searching the shops for a product and wondering why it is difficult to find?

There are many basic items that were readily available, very cheaply, that had an important use in the household. Sadly the drug companies have seen the value in these basic items and have bought them, prohibiting their use except by themselves, spreading fear about each product, sadly believed by many. Many people think that they are being looked after by these companies. This could not be further from the truth. The reality is there is no longer a 'safety net'. However, once you open up to questioning all things, an awareness of the layers of deceit brings realization.

No-one is responsible for you. Humans have survived through the years fending for themselves, growing their own food, making simple creams and potions, using herbs and spices and sharing with others.

Today reliance is upon politicians who are in the pay of the multi-nationals, making laws and regulations to further grow their billion dollar companies. There is no thought about you, no thought about animals, no thought about the planet. Only how to make the most money out of all natural resources, including you.

Products that were once available in every Chemist take some searching out:

Castor Oil and Lugol's Solution of Iodine, plus many more, have almost disappeared.

When you think about it, you will find many basic items, that parents and grandparents talked about, are missing. Add them to the list. You then realise that every one of these products had unique healing properties and were used immediately and with safety. Whereas now, G.P's surgeries are full to overflowing with people waiting for a chemical drug, often for a minor ailment, that could easily be treated at home.

Clean up time – Using your Will

Food has become a challenge. Instead of 'eating to live' many 'live to eat'.

Although necessary for our existence, many people do not know the foods that will keep them healthy. Unfortunately, because of lack of quality, chemicals, artificial substances, sugar content and drugs contained in food, many food sources have become highly addictive dulling our senses.

Depending where you live, Cola is cheaper than water, containing one of the most addictive substances – sugar, triggering the release of opiates in the brain and giving a temporary feel-good feeling. Once it wears off you need another 'fix' – the perfect business!

Pure water is stolen from us and replaced with this addictive substance for which we pay. .Of course, Cola is not the only product to contain sugar ...

Many processed items contain sugar whether sweet or savoury.

Aspartame sweetener is as bad, causing headaches etc. The debilitating effects of Aspartame were researched in Canada during the 1970's/80's but still the product was marketed and has survived to this day!

Richard Wurtman -

a neuroscientist at the Massachusetts Institute of Technology, who studied scores of people who suffered seizures after using NutraSweet, (another name for Aspartame,) says that the likelihood is very strong that aspartame does produce serious and potentially damaging brain effects in a number of people.

Monsanto was the owner of Aspartame products from 1985 – 2000. Since then Aspartame has appeared with several different names including NutraSweet, Equal and Candarel. AminoSweet contains Aspartame – E951, as does NatraTaste and TwinSweet. To avoid Aspartame, check out all new or unfamiliar sweeteners to ensure avoidance.

It is advisable to read all labels, as 'Aspartame' is an added ingredient in many packaged foods and drinks and is not a natural product.

If in doubt, leave it out!

So what can you do to sort out your diet?

It all starts with asking questions, not accepting that advertising holds the truth. Could it be that -

We've been cleverly brainwashed?

Using your Will, you are able to be more resolute, and responsible for your health, telling yourself that 'I Will' rather than taking the defeatist attitude. Improvements are seen as this becomes easier, and the challenge to question all foods and drinks consumed, becomes a way of life. You now use your ability to discriminate and excitedly examine the food as never before.

As simple changes are made, your body 'lightens' appreciating that you are looking after it and making adjustments towards a healthier life.

You learn how to continue to improve your overall health, recognizing when you feel energized and when you feel drained. Your body begins to function more fully and flows with ease.

Food and drink can de-energize the body very quickly leaving room for dis-ease to take hold. Food needs to be fresh and nourishing. After eating, you should feel full of energy, not lethargic or listless.

A classic example is the meal consumed on a Sunday. If you ever feel tired after this large, heavy meal, lovingly called - The Sunday Roast -

this is telling you the foods you have just eaten have depleted your energy leaving you with less energy than before you ate. The digestive system is working overtime to cope with the wrong type of foods and/or the large quantity.

Some schools of thought suggest that space is always left in the stomach at the end of a meal for digestion to take place correctly. This makes sense, rather than eating more than required. The stomach stretches to accommodate unnecessary food, and from that moment, is wanting more food to fill it up.

With the amount of people on the planet right now, this is not a very positive or helpful way to live. When we think of others, all the people who have no food, it is easier to say no to that extra helping, just because it tastes good.

So learning when to stop eating is beneficial and easy to put to action by use of the Will!

And remember, each step gives a positive memory to call upon in the future.

Since the middle of the last century, the rise of technology, chemical drugs, factory pollutants, plastics, decimation of forests, plants, animals, birds and sea-life has made a huge impact on how we view life.

The change has happened so fast, leaving you unaware, until you step back and ask questions, and start to wonder where food actually comes from. The media doesn't help as it is backed by the huge multinational agricultural machine that spits out adverts to sell it's products whilst confusing the people who watch.

Many foods have been advertised as good and necessary one month, followed with opposite descriptions the next. This creation of misleading information worked well for the multinationals. Many people became apathetic, repeating openly that they didn't know what to believe, instead of asking questions and doing their own research.

Very clever marketing - Confusion created! Job done

Your body is the Temple of the Soul and to treat it with respect is the beginning of the journey. Looking at nutrition we find that fruits, vegetables, nuts, pulses and a few grains form the basis of the body's requirements.

24

We have been led to believe that animals and their milks, birds and fishes are necessities for our health. Fortunately, there are many conscious Physicians, obeying the original meaning of the Hippocratic Oath, who are standing up and confirming this to be false. They have seen the disastrous results of animal diets resulting in major illness and disease, the outcome being the use of chemical drugs that never get to the cause.

These Physicians are here to Heal their patients, mind, body and Soul, and they suggest a purely plant based diet. They are totally aware that addiction is a major factor that may be easily overcome once people realise what is happening to them.   This takes just days or weeks to change depending on the individual.

What food would you be unwilling to let go of?

The food or foods you write down will likely be the important ones to stop and the food or drink that is causing stress and dis-ease. It takes only 2 weeks for taste-buds to change but the habit can be stubborn. The mind needs to be checked when you feel yourself giving in to temptation. Use your Will and be strong.

You have strong Willpower and

it is you that must enforce it.

The benefits are greater

than anyone can ever imagine

Chronic Dis-ease

We have all seen friends and family with chronic diseases – including cancers that affect 1 in 4 people. Change of diet takes place when the connection is made of these warnings all around.

Unbelievably, after all the information available about it's power to cause cancer and seeing friends or family suffer hugely, tobacco smoking is still a major habit. Passive smoking can also be a killer.

You can stop, by using your Will. Yes, I know, it doesn't affect everyone, but why take the chance? Do you realise how much your family and friends become concerned knowing you smoke?

A Mum, who had lived through trauma and had a little girl of 5 years old had a shock one day. Her daughter went rushing to her Mummy saying, "Mummy your lung is black, you are going to die". The little girl had seen on television a photo of a lung damaged through smoking. This Mummy told her little girl that all was well and that she would stop smoking at midnight. She did, and never smoked again. She used her Will. This Mummy smoked near on 40 a day!

Yes, this was me! Not proud to have been such a heavy smoker, but extremely proud to have used my Will to stop.

This little girl's concern is an example of how your friends and family are concerned or worried about you, when you smoke. Without you ever knowing.

It is the same today, of course, with diet. There is much information on the importance of cleaning up and eating real, organic food. Watching anyone who is suffering, and not looking after themselves with a good plant-based diet, is a great sadness to the onlooker who cares.

Choices may not be easy to make when you are:

- physically unfit,
- suffering ill-health,
- eating denatured foods,
- holding on to emotions.
- Retaining negative thoughts,
- or bombarded with daily stressors.

However, it is in your own interest to look at the food you are eating as these symptoms may be eradicated by choosing a more nutritious diet. Using discrimination to change, and change quickly, is the most rewarding. Every unhealthy food substituted for a healthy one makes a difference. To do nothing will not mend the problem but will continue fuelling the already damaged body and mind.

Taking action matters.

Your body and mind will appreciate your caring.

There are many so-called 'foods' that are not a necessary part of anyone's diet but have become fashionable to a fault since the restrictions of the 'war-years.' Sweets for instance were non-existent during those war years and many a Granny has been guilty of overcompensating upon her Grandchildren as there were no sweets available for her own.

The well-known dangers from sugar causing inflammation, and artificial colourings being carcinogenic, are at the root of many diseases. Looking back, these origins of problems are easily seen and show us the way forward.

It was also thought that humans needed a high protein diet (taken from research on rats) and people began eating huge amounts of meat and animal products. This proved detrimental not only to animals but to humans causing health problems and obesity.

Humans require 4 – 5% of their total calorie intake per day to be protein. Clearly, this figure can be exceeded - 10% is easily acquired from a whole-food, plant-based diet. Any higher amounts than this and evidence suggests that disease results.

Considering the amount of animal meat eaten, it is no surprise that disease and obesity worldwide have increased dramatically. Peoples who ate very little meat and then partake of a Western diet, full of meat and little else, soon become sickly and develop the same diseases as Westerners, unheard of in their own cultures.

Chemicals and growth hormones given to animals,

end up on the plate, creating a disaster

bringing with it addiction and greed.

"We help people to begin
truly healthful diets,
and it is absolutely wonderful to see,
not only their success,
but also their delight at their ability
to break old habits
and feel really healthy for a change."

Neal Barnard, M.D. -
Physicians Committee for Responsible Medicine.

Part 3

Feeding the Temple

The realization that producers do not have your health in mind when producing food, seems almost fantasy-like to some, akin to science fiction.

The animal agriculture multinationals create a vast production line, treating animals as commodities, having no regard for the sentient beings they are. This cruelty is carried out by humans on behalf of the consumer, permission being given by everyone who eats animal meat. Something most people never think about. That cruelty ends up on a plate intact. Then, it is consumed.

The people carrying out these barbarous crimes have to live with what they have done, and are doing, to sentient beings. Many leave the factory farms and abattoirs, unable to continue the horrific abuse. They later, tell of their own nightmare.

Eating animal meat involves purchasing. Those who do so are complicit in paying other people to carry out torture and killing on their behalf.

It is, a painful story, not one that can be imagined by most.

- Tinned and packaged goods full of carcinogens in the form of additives, with names that are meaningless to the consumer, adorn supermarket shelves. Much time, thought and effort is put into the impact of the packaging.

- Chemical sprays to kill insects and weeds harm not only the target, but are in surrounding crops, filling you with poisons.

- Genetic modification is having many detrimental outcomes when one food is modified with another, confusing to the body and disastrous for those with allergies.

The answer is now visible

Learning more about the way you live your life, and taking responsibility, is vital to your health and well-being. Manufacturers care not for your health or that of the earth, their drive being profit orientated.

30

Many people are sick or overweight, how did it happen?

Write down your own thoughts in answer.

This does not happen overnight, it takes time.   Some sickness is hereditary but only brought about through lifestyle, being one of the reasons some people inherit dis-ease and others do not!

A dampening of the mental ability to say no to foods is borne of chemicals and junk - creating dependency.

What food are you still hanging on to?

Write it down for future reference!

Check again from this list - milk from a cow, manufactured chocolate, cheese, sugary foods, red wine, meat or wheat.

The answer you gave above will be the next one to conquer.

The next time you have a main meal answer the questions below and

Write them down in your journal:

What journey has the food taken from seed or fertilization to plate?

How was it made or produced?

Where in the world did it originate?

What do these strange names mean on the label?

What are the numbers and capital letter abbreviations?

Am I a bystander to cruelty and murder, giving permission for it to exist?

Answer the questions honestly, they are for you alone to contemplate.

The Body Speaks - Learn to listen – we must!

The Four Food Groups

Different foods affect the body:

Think of New Life, as in Springtime

These foods, known as Biogenic, strengthen energy, having the highest Life Force. They are easily digestible with the ability to give new life to the body as it repairs and renews itself.

Think of germinated seeds, sprouted greens such as broccoli shoots, pea shoots, seeds and nuts. Bean sprouts/shoots are familiar from Chinese cooking and also fun for children to watch and take part in, as they grow. This is the newest part of life, containing the highest form of nutrients. A valuable addition to any meal.

Organic fruits and veggies

This is Young fresh Life, Summer

These foods sustain life and are known as Bioactive.

Organic fruits, vegetables and sea vegetables make up the majority of the diet. The fresher the better. The taste of freshly picked fruits and veggies and the energy enhancing quality tells us that this is real food at it's best. Eat as much as you wish.

This is the Mid Life cycle, Autumn

These foods are neutral, known as Biostatic - they usually do no harm but do not improve your energy either.

Raw foods, non organic or not so fresh. Most of the 'fresh' food bought from large super/hypermarkets is transported worldwide, stored and then packaged in plastic. Plastic, that's another subject!

Lightly processed foods also sit here.

The time of Ageing, Winter

Foods and substances that deplete our energy are known as Biocidic - having an adverse effect upon the body.

These foods take your energy down as they are difficult to digest leaving toxins for the body to eliminate. This group includes all processed and irradiated foods and drinks, sugar, all meats, cheeses and dairy.

These wise words on nutrition for humans were first
written, by Professor Edmond Bordeaux Szekely in 1928.
A philosopher and Author of
'The Essene Way: Biogenic Living.'
He also founded the International Biogenic Society with
French Author Romain Rolland -1915 - Nobel-Prize-winner.

"Our adaptation to the natural forces is a
question of existence or non-existence.

We cannot transform the universe or
nature so that they adapt themselves to us;

on the contrary, we must adapt ourselves
to nature and her laws."

--- Edmond Bordeaux Szekely ---

Which foods Can I Eat?

Legumes, Vegetables, Grains, Fruits, Seeds and Nuts

Fruits:

All berries - strawberries, blueberries, blackberries, raspberries. Bananas, apples, pears, melon, watermelon, all citrus fruits and Dried Fruits.

Fruits make up a large portion of your daily intake. Eat a large bowl of mixed fruits for breakfast and take fruits as snacks between meals, particularly mid-afternoon when there is a natural energy dip.

Vegetables:

Greens of all kinds – broccoli, cabbage, sprout tops, chard, spinach, kale. Sweet potatoes, carrots, squash, pumpkin, peppers of colour - green, red, yellow and orange, aubergines, mushrooms, courgettes, cauliflower, asparagus, lettuce, cucumber, olives, avocado, tomatoes, onions, sea veggies. Yes tomatoes are a fruit but work well with all of the above!

A large salad for lunch, lots of veggies at your main meal.

Think colour of the rainbow on your plate!

10 servings of fruits and vegetables rarely leaves any room for any other type of food!

Legumes/Beans/Pulses:

Tofu, soy-milk, peas, beans, lentils, chickpeas, red kidney beans, black-eyed, haricot, butter beans and tempeh.

There are more than 50 varieties of lentils although only 6 to 8 are available to buy, and many different types of beans, nuts and seeds. Each have their own unique flavour.

Whole Grains:

Wheat, bulgur wheat, rye, oats, corn, millet, rice, barley, spelt, durum wheat, buckwheat, pasta.

Grains contain much fibre and keep the intestines - the soil - clean.

Eaten as whole grains instead of refined into flours is even more beneficial if you are able.

Buy organic as much as possible and look to alternatives to wheat as it contains much glyphosate causing many bowel and skin problems to name just two!

Nuts/Seeds and more:

Flaxseed, Chia, Hemp, Sunflower, Sesame, Raw cacao. Walnut, Brazil, Cashew, Almond etc.

Nut butters, tahini - sesame seed spread, nut milks and creams.

Fresh herbs, spices, Himalayan salt, pepper, pickles, onions and garlic turn a meal into a feast!

Questions

Write down the answers in your Journal:

How important is your health to you?

How important to others do you think your health is?

What changes are you willing to make for you

to live a healthy, happy life?

Foods necessary for survival

Simple Meal Ideas

Breakfast:

Oatmeal, banana, berries, apple, nut-milk.

Vary with fruits such as oranges, mangoes, kiwi, pawpaw, fresh figs, dried fruits.

Supplement with raw cacao, cinnamon, mixed seeds, nuts

Lunch:

Large salad comprising: tomato, avocado, lettuce, courgette and carrot – grated, beetroot, red or green cabbage shredded, hummus made with chickpeas and tahini, sprinkle of nuts or seeds.

Add beans, peppers as liked. Lemon juice and Olive oil.

Still hungry - add Tabbouleh made from Bulgur wheat.

Dinner:

Pasta with beans, tomato sauce, garlic, onions, mushrooms, herbs and spices.

This is the time to experiment.

Herbs and spices give the flavour.

Stuff a pepper or aubergine with lentils.

A vegetable curry with rice – add beans or lentils.

A cottage pie with soya mince or beans - add herbs and no-one will know it is solely plant-based.

Serve veggies on the side – broccoli, sprouts, peas, runner beans, kale, carrots, broad beans.

Special Occasions call for a Nut Roast, simple to make and delicious.

Cashews, Brazils, Almonds - take your pick of the many recipes. Decorate with colourful veggies, sliced orange or mint leaves.

Remember pepper and a little Himalayan Salt for extra flavour and Trace Minerals. Yeast Flakes for Vitamin B12 add a cheesy flavour.

The foods above are the mainstay, but you may use plant-based pre-made burgers, sausages, schnitzels, pies, sausage rolls or one of the many products now available.

The list is endless once you find the places from which to purchase.

Snacks:

The easiest of snacks is fruit and nuts, easy to carry and eat anywhere.

Raisins, sunflower seeds, all nutritious. Apples, bananas, kiwi fruits, celery/carrot sticks, a pot of hummus/guacomole.

Wheat:

Bread has not been mentioned as wheat is heavily treated with pesticides, such as glyphosate - the main ingredient in Round-up, causing a reaction in many people, such as bloating, rashes and more. This comes as no surprise when we learn that Round-up decreases the H_3O_2, the essential part of water and plants.

However, there are other grains that are more suitable and include Rye, Spelt flour, Oat flour and Potato flour. Rye and Spelt bread are readily obtainable. If you are avoiding wheat for allergy/health reasons, check the ingredients on the label or ask the baker as many add wheat without declaring it.

A simple recipe for bread is Soda Bread made without yeast.

Wait - there's something missing!

By this time you may be wondering what you may use instead of butter, cream and cheese!

My favourite spread is Coconut oil, whether it is cold and solid or liquid oil, it is great on toast or crackers. Use in mashed potato with a little plant-milk. Olive oil may also be used – it is very much a question of taste. Some are peppery whilst others are subtle and gentle in their flavour. Try several to find the one that suits your palate.

Cream – cashew nut cream may be made. Many creams are readily available, made from oats, nuts or soya.

Cheese – everyone's favourite, except my husband's that is! There is a great variety of ready made plant-based cheeses in the shops and, as always, it is a matter of taste.

Remember, taste buds take a couple of weeks to change (the mind can take longer) so the foods that you may have avoided previously become palatable and delicious.

Cakes, Desserts and more…

There are many delicious recipes for chocolate cakes, fruit cakes and raw desserts if you want to try something different.

Chocolate bars, ice-creams and mousses may all be quite simply made at home – the best use only 3 or 4 ingredients.

They may also be bought in the shops but watch the sugar content - keep them as a special treat!

Maple syrup, coconut sugar or Agave may be used instead of sugar if desired. Dates and bananas add sweetness to many recipes negating the need for extra sweetness.

Nutrition Concerns?

Changing Diet immediately provokes questions from those around, so it is well to be prepared and, more importantly, understand from where nutrients are found.

A well balanced diet includes all Vitamins and Minerals necessary for health and well-being.

However, we are all different, having our own rate of absorption depending on lifestyle, fitness, medications and hereditary factors.

When a plant-based diet is followed, your body tells you what it needs. Generally this takes a while to achieve as the body is recovering from denatured foods, chemicals and general pollution. Once the body becomes 'clean' and all addictions disappear, normality resumes.

This is exciting as the body is now capable of letting you know in advance and helps to prevent colds, viruses and dis-ease.

Some days you may find yourself eating 5 oranges, Hummus with every meal, or, cloves of raw garlic suddenly become attractive, revealing what is required by the body.

The following list of foods is not comprehensive as there are many fruits, veggies, nuts and grains available to us. However, a good selection each day ensures good nutrition.

For pre-existing symptoms make sure you eat extra of the foods indicated.

For instance – my system requires extra Iron, so I ensure I have foods from that group on a daily basis and no longer require supplementation.

Raw Cacao is key, and potent, as are Beetroot and Watercress.

The 4 areas that concern people most are Protein, Calcium, Iron and B Vitamins.

Protein containing foods	Calcium containing foods
Quinoa	Chickpeas
Edamame – Soya	Red Kidney Beans
Spaghetti – Whole Wheat	Almonds, Brazil nuts
Peanut butter	Asparagus
Baked beans	Dried Apricots
Red Kidney Beans	Blackberries
Almonds	Blackcurrants
Broccoli	Oranges
Sunflower seeds	Dark Greens
Sprouts	Tofu
Asparagus	Cinnamon
	Seeds – Sesame, Sunflower

Foods containing Iron

Dark leafy greens
Asparagus
Beetroot
Dried peaches, prunes, apricots
Nuts
Beans and lentils
Kidney beans, Chickpeas
Oatmeal
Raw Cacao

The B-Complex Vitamins

Nuts
Fruits
Brewer's yeast
Brown Rice
Wheatgerm
Green Vegetables
Carrots
Avocados
Cantaloupe
Grapefruit
Raisins
Molasses

Raw Cacao also contains Magnesium. No other food contains as much.

Those chocolate cravings may be real telling you that you require iron, magnesium, or both. As manufactured chocolate does not contain absorbable iron, the body will not benefit - only the craving will be temporarily satisfied. So make sure it is Raw Cacao you are eating to satisfy the body, or the mind will be wanting more.

(A craving has a different feeling or sensation than an addiction. The feeling comes from another place – often the heart area. This may be different for you. It really is an inner knowing that this is needed for your well-being. Once eaten, that's it. There is no craving for more.)

Sprinkle Raw Cacao on muesli, in smoothies - make your own Chocolate delight.

Nutritional Yeast Flakes are Fortified with Vit B12 just to be sure, and to give a cheesy flavour!

Use in cereals, mash, curries, smoothies.

Where to buy

Buying food is dependant on where in the world you live.

Living in or near a city gives access to many supermarkets, most of which carry a range of plant-based foods. These will be frozen for burgers, sausages, quorn and mince - all ideal foods to introduce into your diet, having some resemblance to the foods you are used to consuming. Some supermarkets carry dried foods such as sausage and nut mixes that may be mixed with water before cooking.

Lentils, Chickpeas, Red kidney beans and Baked beans are available in jars or cans. They may also be purchased dried, soaked overnight ready to cook the next day.

Nuts and seeds are usually easy to find.

Organic Markets are the number one place. Find an organic market and you can buy the majority of your veggies and fruits there. Fresh Fruits and Vegetables are also on display in all supermarkets and local markets – organic if possible – in most areas. These comprise the bulk of the food.

Herbs are easily grown in pots indoors or out and add zest to a meal.

Pots on a windowsill or in the garden may contain some greens such as Spinach, lettuce or Chard.

Experiment and enjoy the concoctions you create.

Milks are freely available:

Oat, Rice, Almond, Cashew, Walnut, Soya, Hemp, Spelt and Coconut - Flavours for everyone.

Some very remote areas are quite restricted with the selection of foods available. If this is so, do your best and eat as much variety as possible. Enquire as to the foods of the locals as this can be basic and satisfying.

When travelling it is advisable to carry dried foods and snacks with you.

Simplicity

Food *was* simple and *is* simple but has been made to appear complex with the advent of master chefs turning food into an art form. Although delightful to look at and enjoy, this has had the effect of making food preparation and cooking unattainable, in the minds of many, because of it's complexity - this being the opposite of the intention.

Fortunately there are chefs bringing simple recipes to the fore, educating parents, schools and children that they may eat healthily and simply. This is vital, as to sit and watch a master chef programme, and then order a take-away is most unhealthy!

Many delicious recipes are made of only 4 or 5 ingredients

Avocados, plant milk and raw cacao

Add a little maple syrup, coconut sugar or agave

and you have a delicious **Chocolate Mousse**.

Recipe follows in next section.

Experiment with amounts and adjust to taste.

Food doesn't have to be the same every time,

or have the same name.

'I love my food'.

When referring to something or someone as 'my' this becomes suggestive of 'owning' the subject. Regarding food, in my experience, this is often associated with addiction or habit. The addiction remains unrecognised, but interestingly, reference to cow's milk, cream, cheese, beef and pork are the offenders. All, of which, are known to be highly addictive and harmful to health.

What does this mean to you?

How do you relate to this statement?

Write down your thoughts and feelings on the subject.

Sugar, however, is not usually 'owned' and goes almost unnoticed, veiled from view.

Sugar is a non-food and deprives you of good nutrition. A sweet-tooth needs to be tamed and can be accomplished by gradually cutting it out. A strange thing is that those most addicted think that they do not take much sugar, and have to be reminded of the sugar in all cakes, biscuits, desserts, ices, sauces and pickles - not forgetting the sugar in tea and alcohol.

When you start reading labels, sugar is in almost every product whether sweet or savoury.

A positive gain, when omitting sugar from the diet, is that hundreds of real wholesome flavours begin to reveal themselves!

What a surprise when realisation dawns that all that had been

tasted, until now,

was the overriding sweetness of sugar!

Ingredient check

Making the effort to read the 'Ingredients' list on everything you buy serves you in good stead. If you do not know the identity of the ingredient then don't purchase the product. There are many names on products that are meaningless to most people and these ingredients are often harmful in some way, many being carcinogenic*. Additives of all kinds, written either in numbers or chemical names, confuse the consumer. Many of these, too, are addictive causing highs and lows within the body and creating erratic behaviour.

Carcinogen is a substance that can cause cells to become cancerous by altering their genetic structure so that they multiply continuously and become malignant.

Adelle Davis

- a famous nutritionist

Said that every

teaspoonful of sugar

you give a child

deprives them of good

nutrition.

-This is true not just for children

but for adults as well -

Part 4

Simple Recipe Ideas

As the title says, this is not about recipes, but suggestions to help you use your ingredients without keeping to recipes or names of dishes. This gives basic ideas for you to experiment with. Enjoy - that's what preparing and cooking is all about.

Do you ever decide to make a dish and then realise you don't have the right ingredients? This is very much how I develop new recipes. The key, assuming you want to repeat them, is to write down the alterations or you may not achieve the same result next time. Often the best meals come from no recipe, but looking in the fridge to see which veggies are there, and then in the cupboards for the additions such as chickpeas, nuts or lentils. A little imagination, a few herbs and spices, a touch of confidence, and there's a delicious meal in front of you. If you are unable to repeat the same recipe again – no problem. Use different ingredients and enjoy the new flavours you create.

Quick lunches

Avocado Toasts

Ingredients:

1 Avocado, 1 Tomato, Lemon juice, a little Pepper

2 or 3 slices of thick bread of your choice, toasted. (wheat-free variety)

Washed Lettuce, Baby Spinach, Greens chopped finely,

a few chopped nuts and/or seeds.

Method:

1. Mash Avocado, chop Tomato.

2. Put bread in toaster to toast.

3. While toast is cooking mix Avocado, Tomato and Lemon juice together.

4. Coat toast with olive oil or coconut oil, then spread the Avocado mix on top sprinkling with Cayenne pepper to taste.

5. Garnish with lettuce mix on the plate.

Variation - Use Hummus instead of Avocado. Hummus is easy to make and a good standby. I make batches and store in small containers, for easy defrosting, in the freezer. See next Recipe.

Hummus

A simple recipe with many variations. Add red peppers, turmeric, a spring onion, or parsley and coriander for different flavours. A dash of chilli powder or cayenne pepper gives a little heat. Experiment - it always tastes good.

Base ingredients:

1/3 mug of freshly squeezed Lemon juice

1/3 mug of Olive Oil

1 or 2 tablespoons of Tahini to taste

1/2 teaspoon Himalayan salt

1 teaspoon Cumin (if liked)

4 cloves Garlic

2 cans or jars of Chickpeas, 850gms, or use dried, soaked and cooked.

1 mug of Water - add in last.

Method:

Place all ingredients in a food processor, adding water for correct consistency. I usually add half the water, gradually adding the amount required. Combine all until smooth. Should you add too much water, add more chickpeas.

Place in a serving dish and sprinkle with herbs - mint or parsley - add a dash of Paprika to give a pretty finish.

Use as above instead of Avocado, on crackers or as a dip with raw vegetables such as carrots, celery, cucumber and cauliflower florets. Put a mix of hummus and veggies in a wrap or have a portion of hummus with a salad. Take a pot of hummus with you as a snack or for lunch.

Now you have the main ingredients for any lunch.

For variety, and when you have a little time, roast veggies in a tortilla wrap are delicious and worth the effort.

Roasted Veggie Wraps

(Wraps are usually made from wheat but there are others available. Look for Spelt Wraps as a healthier option.)

Ingredients:

A mixture of veggies of your choice:

Mushrooms cut in half, aubergines sliced or in chunks, cloves of garlic, onions in quarters or chunks. Carrots peeled and sliced, courgettes thickly sliced, red, yellow and orange peppers cut into chunks.

Place all veggies in a roasting tin containing a little oil. Put a tablespoon of olive oil in a dish and add 2 tsp mixed herbs or bouquet garni, a little black pepper and 1/2 teaspoon chilli powder. For extra bite add a little vegan Tamari sauce or Worcester sauce. Drizzle over the veggies. Cook 45 mins at 230C/Gas mark 8. Remove dish from oven and turn the veggies half-way through to ensure even cooking.

When cooked, place a tortilla wrap on a plate. Add veggies through the centre leaving space at one end to fold the tortilla. Add some slices of avocado or mash with a little chilli powder, lemon juice and finely chopped onion. Add a chopped tomato and some chunks of vegan cheese - Egg-free mayonnaise - Hummus - Choose your own extras.

Aim to make more than needed. Then, if there is some left over, use it the next day by warming gently and using in a wrap as before, in ciabatta or on toast.

Soups

Soups are delicious at any time of year. Use any veggies you have. Carrots, celery, tomatoes, chard, spinach, kale, cabbage, onions, stalks of greens, ends of cauliflower, chard, lettuce and celery. Put your chosen veggies in a pot of water and cook for about 30 minutes.

Whizz and add a few herbs, salt and pepper or a little coconut cream sprinkled with fresh parsley.

Be more adventurous and make a Leek and Potato Soup. Simply add chopped leeks and a couple of onions to a pot of water. Add in 3 or 4 potatoes and you have leek and potato soup. Whizz and add a sprinkling of parsley and coconut cream.

A very satisfying soup is made with lentils:

Chop onions, tomatoes and a little garlic to taste. Add to the water in a saucepan. Add lentils of any colour and extra veggies if you like. Bring to boil and simmer until cooked. Leave as is or whizz for a smoother texture. Serve in bowls with chunky home-made soda bread made from rye or spelt flour. If you like curry flavour, a little curry powder is good with this soup.

Add grated vegan cheese or cashew cream to soups, if liked.

Dinner Time

Cottage Pie

- a favourite. Almost indistinguishable from the original. Herbs give the flavour.

1 large Onion chopped

1 Red Pepper chopped

1 Celery stick chopped - if liked

1 Courgette, cut in half lengthwise, then sliced

100g Mushrooms, or other veg such as carrot, chopped

3 Garlic cloves, chopped

225g veggie mince or 100g brown lentils

1 x 400g can chopped tomatoes

1 tbsp Tomato puree

2 or 3 teaspoons Mixed Herbs

Himalayan Salt and pepper

Method:

Heat a tablespoon of olive oil in a saucepan - add onion, garlic and celery, if using. Cook gently for a few minutes. If using veggie mince, add now and cook a little longer. Add the veggies, tomatoes, tomato puree and if using lentils, add now. Season with Himalayan salt and pepper. Add herbs. Cover and simmer for 30 to 40 minutes until cooked. Check every 10 minutes, and if drying out, add a little more water.

Whilst the base of the Cottage Pie is cooking make the following:

Mashed Potatoes:

Potatoes peeled and chopped into equal sized pieces. Boil for about 20 minutes.

Drain and add 2 knobs of coconut oil, a little plant-based milk, salt and pepper.

Thoroughly mash, with a potato masher, until smooth and creamy.

Add more milk if necessary.

When cooked, put the base mixture into a casserole dish and top with the mashed potato. Dot the top with a little coconut oil. Oven bake at 190C/ Gas mark 5 for 30 minutes. Put under grill for extra crispness.

Serve with lightly steamed or boiled greens, broccoli and green beans.

Chilli and Rice

Serves 4

Ingredients:

Rice

1 can tomatoes

1/4 can tomato puree

2 onions, chopped

2 cloves garlic

1 stock cube

1 dried chilli, soaked in boiling water for a few hours

or 1/4 tsp chilli powder - adding a little at a time, making sure it is not too hot.

2 tsp Ground Cumin

1 tsp Paprika

2 tsp Cocoa powder

1 tsp Apple Cider Vinegar

1/2 tsp Himalayan Salt

1 can kidney beans, drained

A few sprigs of fresh Coriander, or use a little dried.

Method:

Put a little olive oil in a pan and saute till translucent.

Add all other ingredients except coriander and beans,

and whiz until smooth.

Simmer for 30 minutes.

Add beans and Coriander and simmer for another half hour.

Whilst Chilli is cooking, cook the rice in boiling water until soft.

Serve: Put rice on a plate and spoon chilli on top.

Decorate with fresh sprigs of coriander, parsley or mint and lemon slices.

(Another time, use more veggies for a different texture and taste.)

Festive Nut Roast

Serves 6

Ingredients:

1 tablespoon Olive Oil

1 onion, chopped

1 clove garlic, sliced finely

2 tsps mixed herbs

2 tsps ground coriander

225g milled nuts (almonds, cashews or a mix)

100g mushrooms, finely chopped

110g wholemeal breadcrumbs

140ml plant milk or water

Salt and pepper to taste.

100g stuffing.

Method:

Heat the oil in a pan and add onion, garlic and mushrooms. Fry gently for 10 minutes but do not allow the onion to brown.

Add herbs and spices.

Stir in the flour and add water/milk gradually.

Cook gently until thickened.

Add nuts, breadcrumbs and seasoning. The mixture should be firm but moist, so add more liquid at this stage, if required.

Make stuffing, if using.

Put half the nut mixture into a well-greased 1kg loaf tin or casserole dish - press down. Spread stuffing mix on top of this, add rest of nut mix and firm. Or without stuffing - put the nut mixture into the dish and press down.

Cover with greaseproof paper, making sure it cannot catch light in the oven, and bake 180C/Gas mark 4 for 1 hour.

To serve:

Turn out onto a large plate and surround with crisp roast potatoes. Decorate with parsley and thin lemon slices.

Serve with cranberry sauce, red currant jelly or apple sauce.

(Not enough nuts - then use more veggies in their place, and a few beans if you wish.)

A Simple Dessert

Here's a recipe for Avocado Chocolate Mousse:

The flesh of 2 ripe Avocados (240g)

½ cup Raw Cacao

1/4 to ½ cup of plant milk

1 tsp pure vanilla essence

1/8 tsp Himalayan salt

2 – 6 tbsp sweetener of choice

Whiz all together adding the milk gradually to form the consistency required.

Put in fridge. Serve with fresh fruits and coconut cream.

A special treat with none of the guilt

or – the phrase often heard:

'I know I shouldn't, but'....

These ideas are to help ease you into a new way of thinking with foods similar in name and taste to those you were used to eating. As changes are made you may find yourself steaming vegetables rather than boiling. Making delicious smoothies, rich in nutrients, becomes a delight for breakfast. Raw foods are more appealing as the taste-buds change and the body feels more alive. The mind is more active and focused, and there is now time to take pleasure from preparing, sharing and eating. A new adventure has begun. The door to a new peaceful world has opened.

Action

Cut out foods
that are not right for you,
or
that you know adversely effect many people.

Maintain a healthy balance.
Include 'foods' necessary for new growth.

Cleanse the 'soil' of your own body
by cutting inflammation causing foods.

Work it until it becomes easy.
Master it.
One step at a time.

This is the base from which to proceed.

Part 5

Physical and Emotional – let's start linking!

The Foundations - How is your soil?

Within the physical body is an area that is referred to as the 'soil'. This is located in the area of the large intestine where the waste from the body passes through. This 'soil' needs cleansing and feeding, creating balance within to keep you healthy. If the soil is not healthy then neither are you.

Plants in poor soil do not thrive but need all the correct nutrients to help them grow. You need the same, good internal soil full of clean, balanced nutrition in order to stay healthy.

This 'patch' is often overlooked and yet many problems stem from the area, affecting the functioning of the brain to the extent of playing a huge part in memory, dementia and depressive states.

If we do not tend our own garden it becomes infested in the form of unhealthy bacteria and parasites, ultimately, adversely affecting all areas of the body.

The Inner Garden

Having seen the 'garden' that nourishes our physical body, we now look deeper. The Inner Garden is a lovely way of looking at physical, emotional and mental disturbances. All are intrinsically linked. Each stage calls for a unique method to clarify dis-ease within the garden. All gardens are different and have their own requirements.

Initially the roots of weeds are unseen, multiplying underground with great speed. Some weeds appear on the surface. You realise that they must be cleared from the garden, before they have a detrimental affect on the beauty of the other plants. You act quickly tugging at them, but forget that the most damage is occurring underground. This quick fix has allowed the roots to proliferate. You revisit the garden and tug yet again, and again but they always return.

Some weeds take longer to appear on the surface. Others continue to grow harmful roots, by spreading for great distances, under the soil.

Some grow abundantly above the surface, binding themselves to every plant within reach. Extremely damaging to plants, they put constant pressure on the fragile stems, suffocating them until they wilt and die.

The challenge of digging deep seemed huge, but looking back what a wonderful transformation is seen.

The birds sing brightly and the tiny creatures visit from time to time thanking you, in their own way, for making the garden full of joy, laughter and happiness.

A worthy job - well done!

You acknowledge, that your own Inner garden can blossom and grow into a space of beauty and peace. You become joyful, and eager to begin or start the search for a Way to clear the Paths leading to it. The wistful thought is: If only I had done this before.....

Now your true journey may begin................

'Hanging on and Letting go'

is associated with the soil in your garden.

Letting go of emotions that are holding you back and clearing the past helps the cleansing process. However, you are still looking at the ground level and the soil. So for this moment diet takes precedence.

Whilst working with this area think about what you may be holding on to that may be harmful.

Hanging on to particular foods because, as a child, they tasted good and re-create memories of childhood. Foods were served with the phrase, 'it's good for you' or you were told that certain foods are necessary for your growth or health.

Hanging on because of fearing changing the diet, or, maybe the thought of any change, makes you fearful.

Hanging on in the mistaken belief that no so-called 'food' is harmful.

Changing what you are eating is the most important step at this time.

So what will I change?

Sugar has already been suggested as it is extremely addictive, stimulating inflammation to create disease of all kinds. The 'soil' becomes disturbed when sugar is eaten, encouraging the growth of unwanted yeasts, and welcoming to parasites.

Cow's Milk is mucus forming, disturbing the equilibrium of the soil and is active in many diseases as seen earlier.

Refer back to the page on diseases and food.

What are the rewards?

- You will feel a sense of achievement that carries into everything you do.
- Personal ideas and dreams become more attainable as your Will becomes stronger.
- Awareness of your body's needs becomes strong and you overcome addictions.
- Each time Discrimination is used to achieve, the stronger the Foundations become.
- Any food that you wouldn't want to stop eating is a good test of the Will!
- Build a positive memory base of Willed achievements.

As your see benefits in your general well-being you investigate to find simple ways to enhance your health and the health of those around you.

Did you know that physically
we have one area to take-in
and seven areas to release?

We take in with the mouth,
and release with the
Anus, Skin, Bladder,
Ears, Eyes, Nose and the Mouth.

When we hold on we may become:
Overweight, have sludgy veins,
produce mucus etc.

More than 60% of
the population are constipated

- that's a lot of holding on!

Constipation

This requires a change in diet, and work on letting go of past traumas and stresses.

Holding on in the form of constipation can be extremely debilitating. Having a direct connection with the brain, mental disturbances and brain 'fog' can ensue. Writing about your past stresses and how you feel deep inside helps the process by eliminating 'emotional waste'. Eat plenty of roughage in the form of greens, veggies and oats. Psyllium Husks also provide a good form of fibre. However, getting to the root of the problem is called for. Physically, you may massage the Fascia Lata - the muscle on the outside of the thigh. Massage with circular movements from knee to top of thigh. This helps the lymphatic system to flow correctly, encouraging the elimination process.

Diarrhoea

This is about giving yourself space. A marvellous period of elimination!

The body takes every opportunity to self-clean. So instead of panicking, be calm. For Diarrhoea take Probiotics - Acidophilus, to increase the good bacteria in the intestine. There are many more natural ways. Drinking plenty of water is necessary to avoid dehydration.

The medical way is to give what I call, 'cloggers'. These medicines clog the system stopping the cold or diarrhoea. The body is then left with the toxins it was trying so hard to help you clear!

There is often a fine line between treating yourself and your family or seeking advice. Never let diarrhoea continue for more than 48 hours, is the general rule, in case dehydration occurs.

Consult a Natural Health Practitioner or your Medic if in doubt. The same rules apply with any illness.

If symptoms worsen, or affect another part of the body, seek professional advice.

Colds

These can be many and varied, requiring different treatments to suit the symptoms. Colds may be a sign that you have been too busy or stressed and that you cannot take any more in – hence the release.

It is said that a 'cold' lasts about three days - should it last longer, then the body takes the opportunity to self cleanse. Think natural remedies, raw fruits and veggies to help the process.

Homoeopathic remedies greatly help:

Pulsatilla 30 taken twice daily for a few days for a cold, or

Belladonna 30 for a high temperature.

See under Homeopathy for more information.

The key is not to panic! Do what you can naturally to help the situation. Should the symptoms go deeper, seek advice.

When you have a 'cold' or diarrhoea, the body may take you through a natural spring-cleaning process. The build-up of toxins has found an escape route!

Your body will always take an opportunity to naturally de-tox

If in doubt consult a professional!

Part 6

Homeopathy

Homeopathy is non-invasive. It stimulates the body's own healing system concentrating on treating the patient rather then Dis-ease.

Homeopathic Law – Like cures Like:

For example if a healthy person survived after eating berries of Deadly Nightshade – Belladonna, they would have a high temperature, be extremely hot, have dilated pupils and burning in the throat and face.

Homoeopathy gives an extremely dilute amount of the substance to a patient exhibiting the same symptoms. So this Homeopathic remedy, Belladonna*, would be used for such symptoms as high dry temperature, sore throat, stings in the mouth, toothache, teething, measles, mumps, scarlet fever, tonsillitis. The remedies are diluted and succussed many times so that none of the actual substance remains. This makes them very potent and with virtually no aggravations.

Here you will find a selection of natural remedies that are most beneficial.

Arnica:

No home should be without it. This is the 'go-to' remedy for many symptoms and situations. Think - falls, scrapes, bruises. Any shock – physically or emotionally. Headache, stings, childbirth. Before operations, dentistry. After surgery instead of painkillers.

Aconite:

Agitation, coughs, colds, chills, sore throats, headaches, earache, toothache, pregnancy, monthly period. Babies teething.

Apis:

Bee, wasp and other insect stings. Inflammation/swelling. Headache, periods.

Arsenicum Album:

Sickness, food-poisoning, indigestion, diarrhoea, coughs, viruses. Useful for illnesses that give no respite as Arsenicum Album helps strengthen every organ of the body.

*Belladonna: – see above.

Bryonia:

Cough, dry. 'Flu, sore throat, indigestion and sickness, headaches.

Cantharis:

Burns, scalds, Cystitis. Mosquito bites. Rash from nettles. Anything causing a burning sensation.

Carbo Vegetabilis:

Food poisoning, drug toxicity, exhaust fumes, gas inhalation. Indigestion and sickness. Toxic headache.

Chamomilla:

Give with Aconite and Belladonna for teething. Calming, soothing.

Gelsemium:

Take before public speaking, exams etc. 'Flu, colds and viruses. Sore-throat, shock. Indigestion and sickness. Headache – feeling of band around head.

Gunpowder:

A blood-purifier. Expels verruchas, warts. Septic conditions, festering.

Hypericum:

Blows to fingers, toes or spine. Painful cuts or wounds. Can be taken for tooth extraction and fillings. Horse-fly bites. Anything affecting nerve endings.

Ignatia:

Nervous shock. Indigestion and sickness. Headache, convulsions. The remedy for the shock of loss – grief.

Merc. Sol:

Chills, colds, 'flu and viruses. Sore throat, earache. Catarrh greenish. Mercury is contained in most old fillings of the teeth and leaks into the mouth and body. Mercury may be taken for signs of gum ulcers, sores or metallic taste in the mouth.

Nux Vomica:

Vomiting, over-indulgence, indigestion, toxic headaches, convulsions.

Pulsatilla:

Coughs after a virus. Measles, indigestion and sickness, headache, earache, mumps. Pregnancy and periods. Weepy.

Rhus Tox:

Pains round joints, worse from movement. Stiffness, restlessness. Worse in damp, cold.

Ruta:

Eye strain. Strained tendons. Bones feel bruised.

Symphytum:

To mend broken bones. Injuries from a blunt blow to the eye.

Cold and Flu Prophylactic:

(New strains each year, commencing September/October). Boosts the Immune System to lessen the chance of manifesting 'flu's and viruses.

These remedies may also be used for your animal friends in time of need. I've personally used homeopathy on many animals including horses, dogs, cats, rats, birds and monkeys with great success. Even your plants and trees benefit from an occasional dose. For example when moving a plant from one location or pot to another give one dose of Arnica to help with the shock of disturbing them.

Useful Topical Creams and Ointments:

- Calendula Cream for healing cuts and grazes.
- Hypericum Ointment for Injuries to areas rich in nerves. Spine, toes, fingers. Painful wounds.
- Arnica Cream for pain relief from bruises. Can reduce swelling and discolouration. Muscle pain and weakness.

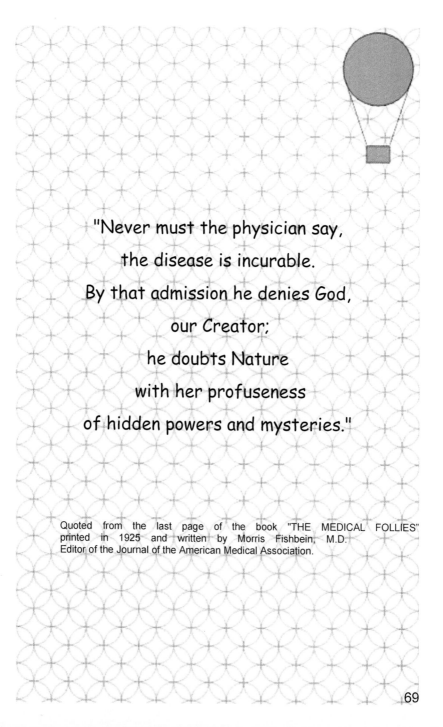

"Never must the physician say,

the disease is incurable.

By that admission he denies God,

our Creator;

he doubts Nature

with her profuseness

of hidden powers and mysteries."

Quoted from the last page of the book "THE MEDICAL FOLLIES"
printed in 1925 and written by Morris Fishbein, M.D.
Editor of the Journal of the American Medical Association.

Bach Flowers

The Bach Flower Remedies help balance the whole person, similarly to homeopathy. These may be used safely for self-healing yourself, family and animals that choose to live with you.

These beautiful flowers bring back calm, peace, happiness and enthusiasm, once hidden by negativity. There is a line of balance between negative and positive aspects. The Bach flowers bring you back to a state of equilibrium. The positive aspects are written below in italics.

There are 7 headings with brief descriptions of the dual aspects of each remedy.

Remedies for Fear

Aspen:

Vague, unknown fears. Terrified something terrible may happen. Afraid to tell others.

Faith to invite new experiences and adventure.

Cherry Plum:

Desperate, suicidal. Fear of the thought of losing control.

Calm, quiet courage and sanity.

Mimulus:

Shy, timid, knows the fears.

Brings back courage and understanding.

Red Chestnut:

Fearing for others, projecting the worst. Over-care and concern.

Trusting that life will show the way. Calm in an emergency.

Rock Rose:

Extreme fear, alarmed, intensely scared, dread.

Courage to face emergencies. Selflessness.

Remedies for Uncertainty

Cerato:

Self-distrust. Repeatedly seeking advice. Foolishness.

The ability to choose the correct action. Intuitive.

Gentian:

Pessimism, doubt. Depression from known cause.

Optimistic and persevering with all action.

Gorse:

Hopelessness, despair, pointless to try.

Certain difficulties will be overcome. Positive faith.

Hornbeam:

Tiredness, weariness, doubts own strength. Monday morning feeling.

Sure of own ability. Supportive.

Wild Oat:

Uncertain which path to follow. Drifting.

Definite ambitions and sure of purpose in life.

Lack of Interest in the Present

Chestnut Bud:

Failing to learn from mistakes. Repeats same mistakes. Lacks real observation.

Keenly observant. Keeping focused in the present.

Clematis:

Day-dreaming, absent-minded, inattentive

Back down to earth. Artistic and inspired.

Honeysuckle:

Living in the past memories. Homesick.

Retains wisdom of the lessons and lets go of the experience.

Mustard:

Deep depression, black cloud appears suddenly.

Clarity, Inner serenity and Joy.

Olive:

Exhausted, no more strength after long period of suffering.

Peace of mind. Strength to overcome difficulties.

White Chestnut:

Thoughts go round and round. Mental arguments.

Quiet, calm mind. Undisturbed by outside influences.

Wild Rose:

Lack of interest, resignation. Apathy.

Lively interest in all things.

Loneliness

Heather:

Talkative bore, longing for company. Concerned only with self.

Selfless, inspiring in efforts to help. Understanding.

Impatiens:

Irritated by constraints, quick, tense. Dislikes interference.

Great gentleness, understanding and tolerance of others.

Water Violet:

Proud, reserved, aloof, feels superior.

Sympathetic wise counsellors. Learns from experience.

Oversensitivity

Agrimony:

Worry hidden behind a brave face. False smile.

Can truly laugh at their own problems. Optimistic, peacemakers.

Centaury:

Weak-willed, over-anxious to please. Easily exploited.

Quiet, wise, serving. Knowing when to give or not.

Holly:

Jealousy, anger. Lack of love for fellow men.

Generous, loving, tolerant. Love is key.

Walnut:

Oversensitive to strong outside influences. All changes.

Follows beliefs perseveringly. The link breaker.

Despondency and Despair

Crab Apple:

Feels unclean. Self-disgust. Small things out of proportion.

The Cleansing Remedy. Broad-minded, seeing things in perspective. Control of thoughts.

Elm:

Capable, but overwhelmed by responsibility.

Performs duty with strength. Confident, self-assured.

Larch:

Fear of failure. Lacking in confidence and Will to succeed.

Willing to try, and not discouraged by failure.

Oak:

Struggling and plodding against the odds. Persistent, not giving in.

Admitting limitations. Stable and courageous.

Pine:

Guilt, self-reproach, over conscientious, takes blame for others mistakes.

Perseveres with humility. Helps where possible, does not dwell on mistakes made.

Star of Bethlehem:

All forms of shock, sorrow, grief. Physical, mental and emotional.

Clears body and mind of the tensions and residues of shock.

Sweet Chestnut:

Anguish, desolation.

Faith in spite of anguish. Desire and understanding to help others.

Willow:

Poor me, life is unfair. Resentment, bitterness.

Uncomplaining. Realises the power of thought to attract good or bad.

Over-care for Others' Welfare

Beech:

Intolerant, Critical, Arrogant, Judgemental.

Seeing good all round, and perfect tolerance.

Chicory:

Demanding, self-pity, possessive, tearful. Craves attention.

Truly selfless in care and concern for others.

Rockwater:

Self-denial, rigidity, self repression, likes to set an example.

Idealist with flexible mind. Ability to enjoy experiences in life.

Vervain:

Over enthusiastic, causing strain and stress. Incensed by injustices.

Calm and sure of mind. Quiet and tranquil.

Vine:

Domineering, inflexible, ambitious, strong.

Wise, understanding leader. Guide and help for others. Great strength.

The Bach Flower Remedy to carry with you:

Rescue Remedy

Five of the 38 remedies form the famous Rescue Remedy, or 5 Flower Remedy, that has a home in many a handbag and kitchen drawer:

Comprises:

Cherry Plum, Clematis, Impatiens, Star of Bethlehem and Rock Rose.

Use for any emergencies and accidents, first aid, sudden difficulty. Mentally, emotionally or physically.

Very fast, Powerful.

Vitamins and Minerals

As seen in the food section, all vitamins and minerals may be obtained from a plant-based diet. Unlike animal-based diets there is no extra waste for the body to dispose. This leaves the body free to absorb the nutrients without any interference or delay.

However, because many of us are changing our ways and ate animal products in the past, it is advisable to supplement in short spurts to give the body a boost, just as would happen if we lived in nature when all the berries or carrots ripened at once. This would be our mainstay at that time wouldn't it?

Having orange and grapefruit trees in my garden is an example as I have grapefruit daily and five or more oranges in one day when all ripen at once. A great natural boost of Vitamin C and other minerals.

Vitamin C and Iron

With this in mind, supplementing with Vitamin C just before the cold season makes sense.

Iron supplementation may be taken alongside Vitamin C as this aids absorption of the Iron.

To obtain Iron, in the past, it was usual to put a nail through an apple and leave it overnight. In the morning the nail was taken out and the apple eaten complete with the iron residue from the nail. The Vitamin C in the apple allowed full absorption.

Vitamin B12

This vitamin sees many people deficient. It has been said that vegetarians and vegans need to make sure they take a supplement as they are unable to acquire it from their diet. However, this is not peculiar to vegetarians and vegans, as many eating an animal based diet also require a supplement. It is probably unnecessary to take B12 all the time but to have a routine of taking it periodically, just in case.

Vitamin D3

Important if you do not go outside daily. Vitamin D3 is made by the body naturally, when exposed to the sun. Many people are unable to go into the sun because the rays are too fierce now, so supplementation may be required.

In the past, children would develop Rickets - they often had bow shaped legs in adulthood.

Nowadays we see much osteomalacia and osteoporosis in adults. Staying indoors is one reason Rickets has re-appeared. The other reason being the high consumption of cow milk. Humans are unable to absorb calcium from this animal milk and end up losing calcium from the bones instead of replacing it.

Vitamin D3 – the best form – made from Lichen, is the most natural and easily absorbed. This contributes to maintaining bones, muscle function, the immune system and teeth.

As shown earlier, there are many chemicals, drugs, plastic fibres, hormones and pesticides in foods. These have an impact on our Immune Systems, making it necessary to supplement, in order to maintain good health, and prevent dis-ease. Once the system is 'clean' and fresh, toxins eliminated and organic foods consumed, it may not be necessary to supplement so much.

At the first sign of lethargy, breathlessness or aches and pains, with no obvious reason, it may be advisable to take Vitamins, particularly Vitamin C, to give the immune system a boost.

As always, seek information from your Natural Health Care Practitioner or a Medic if in doubt.

Colloidal Silver

This is a fabulous remedy to have in the cupboard.

Silver has been used as an anti-bacterial and anti-viral long before anti-biotics. Silver is also used in space by NASA.

A thousand years ago a Cholera outbreak was avoided by those who could afford to eat their food with a silver spoon..

- Colloidal Silver is easily obtainable.
- An effective agent against bacteria and viruses. (Like an antibiotic, it will also decrease the good bacteria in the gut. So balance with Probiotics.)
- Use it topically for mosquito or insect bites.
- Cat scratches.
- Open wounds and grazes.

- It is great for animals too. Used topically and quickly, sees wounds heal without the need for a trip to a vet. For an animal that is afraid to come close, I have used a dropper or a spoon and thrown the silver on a wound. The wounds heal.

You will find that many natural remedies work well together. Do some research, so that you are prepared for diverse situations, and you will be pleased you did, as you and your family maintain good health.

As with all health issues it is important to look at the body, mind and Spirit as a whole, as each affects the other. Natural remedies, particularly Homeopathy, look at the person as a whole.

Part 7

Discrimination

Taming our Inner world may begin with the physical level, overcoming aches and pains, discovering the right foods for you, and taking regular exercise. All have an impact on the whole Being.

Starting with the physical, using DISCRIMINATION and setting the WILL in motion.

- When anxious, depressed, under stressful conditions or situations, benefit comes from a tangible force on which to concentrate.

- Good foundations, better health, positivism and a sense of achievement, prepare the way.

- It is then that other areas may be looked at as the body becomes physically stronger.

- Focusing on achieving better health and well-being satisfies the mind and allows for a calmer outlook on life.

- The negative impact of stressful situations is lessened as better choices are made.

- Clarity abounds and suppressed parts of the psyche float to the surface and clear.

Therefore working with diet and exercise, emotional levels are activated and with the use of positivity many hidden forces may be eradicated.

The physical is a mirror of the emotions and carries memory of all experiences within.

Discrimination is one of the Cosmic Laws

What does the word mean to you?

How will you put it into practice?

Write your thoughts and feelings in your journal.

WILL POWER

Are you aware of saying or thinking: 'I don't have the willpower to do that'?

It is a common phrase spoken or thought - too often, too lightly.

Think and write down all times you have used this phrase or similar.

How will you now put your Willpower into practice?

Write down in your journal as a reminder for future reference to see how far you have moved on.

Confidence Balance Fun Challenge

- Physically, exercise strengthens the muscles and improves balance.

- Exercise keeps you in shape for those sudden times when you are called upon to use more strength than usual.

- Exercising Willpower to overcome and move through physical exercise creates gain in the knowledge that you have proven to your-self that achieving is possible.

You are building new positive memories for the future. This leads on to other patterns in life urging you to use the Will to move through and conquer addictions, fears, stubbornness and apathy. You are building a list of achievements, however tiny. Tiny steps on a daily basis, creating solid foundations.

What are the benefits of exercise emotionally and mentally?

How may this help you?

Write them in your journal.

All the while we are in non-active mode struggling with everyday occurrences, eating without thinking, lacking in exercise, suffering from general malaise, lacking enthusiasm, depending on alcohol, social media, television and other screens – progress can stagnate.

Once action is taken, with routines and good habits in place, pressure dissipates leaving freedom to move forward to deeper aspects of the Self. Habits take 30 days to form and many of these last a lifetime. Some are worthy of keeping and nurturing whilst others have no place in our life, but were borne from denial, brainwashing or copied from others without question.

Copying

An example of copying is the teenager who wants to belong to the crowd, so partakes of cigarettes, drugs or alcohol. This type of copying leads to dependency. Children copy their parents and form good habits such as personal cleanliness. However, bad habits are copied too.

Habits that form into addictions,

cause health problems in the future.

Everyone has habitual behaviour worthy of investigating and changing where applicable.

Which habits do you wish to change?

Are there good, worthy habits you would like to form?

Write lists in your Journal and monitor your progress from time to time.

Exercise .... helping the physical, with a bonus affect on the emotional and mental.

What are you drawn to?

Look at various themes and choose one that you feel will work for you, at this time. Stay with that until you are confident of the improvement and then change to another exercise regime. Nothing is set in stone, so be accepting of where you are and accepting of change also.

Diagram of Back Muscles

- based on an old, antique wooden statue.

When you feel a twinge or ache it is useful to check with the diagram to define the shape of the muscle. There is then a sense of the muscles' whereabouts whilst exercising, and generally moving about.

(This muscle model is a fun diagram.

If you prefer you may look in any anatomy book and find a more sober picture.)

Exercise for All

Chi Gong

If exercise is lacking because of illness or overweight you may wish to start with the gentle exercise of Chi Gong. Chi Gong helps awareness of the energy around and within you, and awareness of the worth of creating stillness and calm inside.

Start gently, sensing the energy moving through the body. The body gradually comes back to balance. All exercise needs regularity to achieve worthwhile results.

(Recommended: Lee Holden – Chi Gong)

Planks

A magical exercise building confidence as well as balance. Maybe 6 seconds on the knees is the starting point. No matter, gradually increase to 45 seconds daily taking a break every fourth day.

No time at all for great rewards. Take time to build the seconds. There are formulas to follow. Find one that is simple.

Diamond Dallas Yoga

Exercise using Dynamic Resistance is now my go to of choice, most days exercising in the mornings before breakfast. This is not yoga in the true sense, but takes the moves and turns them into a powerful form of exercise to strengthen each muscle. Uses dynamic resistance, also known as Isometric exercise. Even those who have not exercised at all are able to gain from this. You 'make it your own', working at your own pace, improving and strengthening by the day.

Start gently, becoming aware of your body. Sense the muscles switching on and getting stronger. Using the diagram to locate each muscle is fun. You begin to see and feel the location of each, and how well they are functioning. A whole body workout or a section at a time. The choice is yours!

(Diamond Dallas Yoga – DDP Yoga)

(If you have a serious disability - this is not for you. Always consult your health provider if in doubt. This is not for everyone. If this is the case,

you may wish to use your Will in different ways to help your own journey. Some of the self-disciplines noted below may be adapted to suit your requirements emotionally or mentally.)

All this may be done at home – and that is where Willpower really comes into it's own.

Self-discipline means work for most people. So one way to 'make this happen' is to have a routine:

Every night before bed, reinforce your intention by entering in your diary the next workout, and what you would like to achieve. Put a note on the wall in the kitchen, to remind you to drink a glass of water before you start.

Allowing obstacles to invade this few minutes space of the day is then simply avoided. Once the habit has formed you will fly - enjoying the benefits of feeling fit. There are some who do not need these reminders. Once their mind is set they continue on regardless.

Find your routine, stick with it, have fun and laugh loads.

The other way is to find a local class to attend, of which there are many. Look for one of greatest benefit, working all the muscles.

There are many forms of exercise

Here are some others you may like:

Yoga, Pilates, Zumba, Tai Chi or Keep Fit,

as well as dancing, jogging, running, and

sports, such as football, tennis, badminton,

swimming and more.

Brisk walking is beneficial.

Swinging arms and focusing on how you walk. Make sure that your right arm and left leg are forward at the same time and vice versa, to ensure both sides of the brain are functioning optimally.

Start with one and if you enjoy it, stay, if not look elsewhere for something more suitable.

Mix them up – swimming, running and Pilates.

Find your favourites and go for it!

Sometimes muscles remain active instead of switching off. This happens when they are protecting an injury, minor or major. The injury may have happened recently, or in the past. The body is protecting the damaged muscle but has not switched back to normal. It seems that these muscles are the problem. In some cases, feathering the tight muscles will help. A light tickle in the centre gives permission to the muscle to relax.

If you think the muscle has switched off, you may gently massage each end, gently pushing towards the belly of the muscle. The diagram will help you locate the ends of the muscle, or look it up in an anatomy book.

The tickle method may also be used for cramp. Tickling or feathering the centre of the muscle and then the whole area of discomfort.

At other times emotional tension in the past or present may be the culprit as memory is stored in every cell of the body, making muscles a good storehouse and place of information.

Negativity also dispels energy and this results in tiredness and pain. When there is an ache in the back, shoulder or neck it can be a reminder of a memory, or of behaviour patterns that require addressing. This is not obvious until, whilst exercising, a distant memory may come to the fore for no apparent reason. If so allow it to surface, acknowledging it is there. Often the memory passes through as though it is being shown to you and then moves away. This is the beginning of letting go of the junk leading on to digging deeper!

A great way to get fit and clear some baggage at the same time!!

The effect of exercise mentally, can be immense as the mind becomes clearer, more alert and focused. Muscles of the brain and the lymphatic system benefit from exercise allowing flow rather than stagnation.

Using the Will and Discipline to conquer the mutterings of 'can't do it' or 'can't be bothered' is a win, win situation.

(Disclaimer: This book contains many ideas that work for many people and is not suggesting that you start any exercise routine or any other discipline, including dietary changes, without doing your own research or contacting your Health Professional)

Gratitude

I awake in the morning
full of gratitude for the new day
and the many wonders it will bring.
Tomorrow is the day
that isn't here or there.
It rests in the darkness
enjoying the limitless interval
and takes it's time
to expand into full beauty.

Hazel Humble

A Challenging Situation

each of us face whatever beliefs are held right now.

This little story, from my own experience, may be applied to many diverse situations.

The deepest hurts, feelings and beliefs are often kept hidden. Never spoken about. This breeds confusion in all areas, no matter what the issue. Lack of communicating and just 'getting on with it' results in 'bad feeling' as no-one can possibly see what lies beneath.

The inclusion of this is to shed Light on a particular type of suffering that you may share. Understanding the feelings that come to the fore, in the following situation, helps general interaction and encourages mindfulness.

Sharing your own thoughts, especially if you are living with someone who has no idea of your deepest feelings, helps ease the tension. Once out in the open people have a chance to understand.

Imagine you have decided that the time is right to change your diet to plant-based.

You begin your journey with apprehension, uncertain of how you will survive. Food is not the issue, but how people will respond to you. Very soon, you find that people react with cognitive dissonance. They feel that their way of life is under threat.

To cover their guilt they become very concerned about your health. Yet another way of making you feel awkward and even upset. They have never thought about the nutrition, or lack of it, on their own plate. A deep sadness overcomes you as you try to explain. It manifests as anger giving them something they can understand.

You have fallen into the trap. You are now seen as highly emotional or irrational, and they are happy as they no longer have to look at themselves. The true feelings that manifested immediately you said you eat plant-based, block. Back they go into the 'box.'

Eating out

Everyone at the table places an order containing meat.

They are all eating animals! All salivating about the dead lamb, dead pig and slaughtered cow, without realising how very deeply you hurt, and how much you care. You have researched into the 'food' animals they are eating. Looking behind the scenes revealed the reality. The reality was unbearable.

Screams of fear, pain and loss come alive as you watch your dear ones eating. They are completely unaware of what you are hearing and seeing. You see the animals with fear in their eyes. They lived through torture, cruelty and emptiness. Never experiencing freedom, they are now on a plate. False advertising shows cows, sheep and pigs grazing in fields. The horrors of the farming industry concealed.

Yes, there are some farms like this but cows still have their babies taken away. All end up at the slaughterhouse, seeing their friends killed and knowing they are next in line. You hear their cry and bellowing as someone orders veal. The wailing is exactly as we would if someone took our baby. You see the baby, in the dark, in a small crate with no light, knowing that there they stayed for three months before being slaughtered. They never experienced life with their Mother or ran free on grass and earth.

You care deeply, and once shown the truth, had no choice but to take action and reassess your lifestyle. You feel so sad and completely alone. Quietness sets in as you become uneasy, waiting to hear the same questions again. You try to answer but the images take over. You have cried tears of sadness or covered the tears with anger, many times.

The conversation turns to cats, dogs and horses. Suddenly, everyone is cooing about their pets and saying how much they love animals. You begin to feel quite ill, whilst listening to the inconsistent chatter, schizoid in content.

To mention that they are sentient beings, as the animals on their plate, would be seen as an intrusion. Experience informs you that anger and ridiculous statements will be thrown your way. You feel more and more uneasy, listening to this bizarre talk.

(Schizoid means disassociation)

You wonder how, whilst eating an animal, in the same breath, people can talk about loving animals. You remind yourself that you were the same once, cut off from feeling whilst eating animal flesh. Yet, when light was shone into the darkness and horror revealed, you did your own research.

Someone asks if your meal is good. What do you say in response? Most of the time the meal is acceptable. Your only concern is that it will be completely plant-based. Even though basic, that is of no importance.

The chef is often not educated about nutrition, and presentation is lacking. Supplementation at home has become normal.

At last, everyone stops discussing the animals on their plates. You breathe a sigh of relief as the conversation changes.

The Opponent is your Friend

In moments of pain such as this, remember the adversary is there to make you stronger. Sometimes, silence speaks louder than words. Take encouragement as you see the calmness, mindfulness and respectfulness growing within you.

You are all at different stages on this journey. Take this opportunity to show gratitude for where you are at. It takes time, but you work to be strong enough to sit through it. Then, in a quiet moment, state your case with gentle passion. Speak the truth, and then, let it go. Education is the key as the veil of secrecy implemented by law in many countries is immense. If it is appropriate, you will find an opportunity to speak one to one, from the heart. The person will hear you, and understand your strong ethics that come from the deepest Truths.

If you eat plant-based you may wish to share this with your loved ones who do not eat plant-based. This will help them understand a little of how you feel. If you are a carnist, however, reading this will give insight into feelings you have never experienced. In this way, compassion is enabled.

Extenuating circumstance may make the change less easy, for some. Acknowledge this and look deeper to see what may be holding them back.

There is no need to compromise your ethics, but walk side by side

When other people seem stuck or even uninterested, try 'putting yourself in their shoes' for a while. There may be something you can help them with. This doesn't always mean helping with dietary change. Easing their life a little by listening, or helping out in some way, may suffice. Then let it go. There is no benefit in 'hitting a brick wall'. Sow the seed and walk away.

This approach certainly worked on me, once I was told about the horrors of the animal agriculture business. I was vegetarian for many years as were my children. When confronted with the information I was convinced that I would never become Vegan, still in denial of what I had heard. It couldn't possibly be that bad, surely? Even with my experience that 'everything from the cow' was the number one cause of ill-health.

However the very next time I went shopping, I found myself putting the yogurt back on the shelf. I could no longer eat it. The same gradually occurred with eggs, the little milk I used, cream, cheese and chocolate. My Soul had other ideas. Thankfully, I was not stubborn enough to ignore this huge 'message', seemingly arriving from the yogurt pot! My life changed considerably from that moment. Researching, digging deeper within and discovering much that had been previously hidden from my sight.

The outer world changed as well as the Inner. A veil had been lifted creating Freedom from a guilt of which, until then, I was unaware.

We remain unaware of the weight we carry until it has gone.

The Soul or Higher Self guides us, in it's own time, despite all our excuses… when we are ready to listen.

Should you be working through the book and are unable, at this time, to move forward:

- *Ask yourself questions about why change seems unimportant or too challenging, remembering that everything we do or choose not to, has an impact on those around us and our Mother – Planet Earth.*

- *Re-read this again to find the areas that provoke deeper feelings. Take time to recall from whence is their origin.*

- *Take space enough to meditate or contemplate the issues arising.*

- *Then work them through using your notes from the journal.*

The powers of Discrimination and Will are always at your command. Use them wisely.

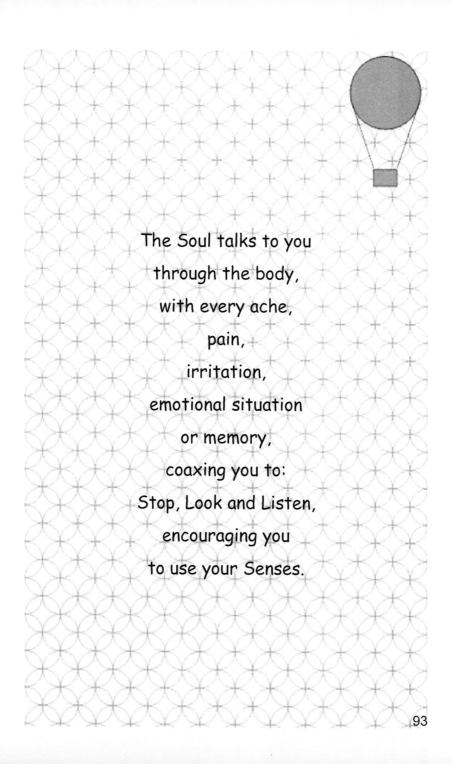

The Soul talks to you
through the body,
with every ache,
pain,
irritation,
emotional situation
or memory,
coaxing you to:
Stop, Look and Listen,
encouraging you
to use your Senses.

Further Information, References and helpful sites:

Hyperactive Children's Support Group
71 Whyke Lane, Chichester, PO19 7PD, United Kingdom

Josie Du Toit - Plant-based Health Coach,
(Recovered herself from Fibromyalgia and Chronic Fatigue.)
josievegan@outlook.com

In depth information on Homeopathy -
Materia Medica by William Boericke M.D.

Homeopathic Remedies -
Galen Pharmacy, Dorchester, Dorset.
Helios Homeopathy - https://www.helios.co.uk

Healing Herbs of Dr. Bach
https://www.healingherbs.co.uk

The Vitamin Bible, by Earl Mindell - available on Amazon,
 for simple Information on vitamins.

Colloidal Silver -
https://www.herbwisdom.com

'Touch for Health' Paperback – 2012
By John Thie and Matthew Thie
A Practical Guide to Natural Health with Acupressure Touch and Massage

Information on how to keep hydrated -
h3o2water.com